The Divine Dance of Love

Sharing in the Mystery of Christ

CHRISTOPHER COLLINGWOOD

Foreword by

MARTIN ISRAEL

The Canterbury Press
Norwich

British Library Cataloguing in Publication Data

A catalogue record for this book is available from the British Library.

ISBN 1-85311-146-5

*Typeset by David Gregson Associates, Beccles, Suffolk
and printed in Great Britain
by Biddles Ltd, Guildford and King's Lynn*

FOR

SUE
BEN
ANDREW
DOMINIC
AND
TERESA

CONTENTS

FOREWORD

This is a very beautiful account of the events of Christ's life, recounted in a carol called *My Dancing Day*, the authorship of which remains unknown. It first appeared in a collection made by William Sandys and was published in 1833. It seems strangely appropriate that this beautiful piece remains authorless, for its fabric is as delicate as a spring flower, strong to the cold but fragile to insistent investigation that would find no use for poetry like this, other than its selling value.

As Christopher Collingwood reminds us, there are two movements intrinsic to the dance: a linear progress and a spiral, or cyclical advance. We all have to experience these two motions to attain completeness of life on earth, and Jesus, who showed us the way forward, was the perfect exemplar of both of them. The dance, furthermore, involves the entire body, reminiscent of the body of Christ, and its full character is revealed as we lose ourselves in the pleasure of our partner and the fully accepting love of God. He is indeed the Lord of the Dance, and in his embrace we find warmth and direction, peace and wisdom.

A particularly important chapter in this book is 'Religionising'. It implies a deep distrust of popular religion with dogmatic overtones. This was a temptation laid at the feet of Jesus: had he opted for a nationalistic kingdom such as the devil offered him, he might have reached great pinnacles of power (with a small group of the elect to accompany him), but the world would have remained unchanged. However, Jesus opted for the way of a larger vision, and although he died in agony, he set in motion a new age of humanity that is only now, two thousand years later, beginning to take root – and this applies

to so-called Christian groups in Northern Ireland and
Bosnia among many other people in the world. I welcome
Christopher Collingwood's courage in mentioning this
quite candidly as he gives pleasant vignettes of the religious views and actions of his growing family, four
delightful children to whom, together with his wife, the
book is dedicated.

The final four chapters deal with the ultimate questions
of suffering, dying, rising, and realising, after which there
is a beautiful final prayer. It is only nine lines long, but it
serves to bring the Holy Spirit, Christ, and the Father into
one glorious Trinitarian whole.

MARTIN ISRAEL

ACKNOWLEDGEMENTS

There are a number of people without whose assistance the writing of this book and its preparation for publication would have been much harder, and I am delighted to be able to express my gratitude to them:

My colleagues and the people of St Paul's, Bedford, who made it possible for me to be away from the parish in order to write the book in the first place.

Mother Anne SLG of the The Convent of the Incarnation, Fairacres, Oxford, who agreed so readily to my request to spend two months living at the Convent of St Mary and the Angels, Hemel Hempstead, and Sister Susan SLG and the other members of the community, who allowed me the rare privilege of sharing so deeply in their life together, and whose prayerful support and interest in the book was such an encouragement.

My parents, who enabled me to be reunited with my family at weekends in their home during the same period;

Susan Rees, who typed up the manuscript, and whose patience, generosity and sheer professionalism at every stage made all the difference in the world.

Friends, who read the typescript and made helpful comments and suggestions: David Mainwood, Judith and Stewart Munday, and Alison Considine and Angela Tilby especially, both of whom took a particular interest, and who cannot possibly be aware of the extent of my gratitude.

Martin Israel, who has been a constant friend and guide, who encouraged me to begin the process of writing, and who so generously offered to write a foreword.

Lastly, my wife, Sue, who knows just how crucial her love and support is to me.

MY DANCING DAY[1]

Tomorrow shall be my dancing day:
I would my true love did so chance
To see the legend of my play,
To call my true love to my dance:
Sing O my love, O my love, my love, my love;
This have I done for my true love.

Then was I born of a virgin pure,
Of her I took fleshly substance;
Thus was I knit to man's nature,
To call my true love to my dance;
Sing O my love, O my love, my love, my love;
This have I done for my true love.

In a manger laid and wrapped I was,
So very poor, this was my chance.
Betwixt an ox and a silly poor ass,
To call my true love to my dance:
Sing O my love, O my love, my love, my love;
This have I done for my true love.

Then afterwards baptized I was:
The Holy Ghost on me did glance,
My Father's voice heard from above,
To call my true love to my dance:
Sing O my love, O my love, my love, my love;
This have I done for my true love.

Into the desert I was led,
Where I fasted without substance;
The devil bade me make stones my bread,
To have me break my true love's dance;
Sing O my love, O my love, my love, my love;
This have I done for my true love.

The Jews on me they made great suit,
And with me made great variance.
Because they loved darkness rather than light,
To call my true love to my dance:
Sing O my love, O my love, my love, my love;
This have I done for my true love.

For thirty pence Judas me sold,
His covetousness for to advance;
'Mark whom I kiss, the same to hold,'
The same is he shall lead the dance:
Sing O my love, O my love, my love, my love;
This have I done for my true love.

Before Pilate the Jews me brought,
Where Barabbas had deliverance;
They scourged me and set me at nought,
Judged me to die to lead the dance:
Sing O my love, O my love, my love, my love;
This have I done for my true love.

Then on the cross hanged I was,
Where a spear to my heart did glance;
There issued forth both water and blood.
To call my true love to my dance:
Sing O my love, O my love, my love, my love;
This have I done for my true love.

Then down to hell I took my way
For my true love's deliverance.
And rose again on the third day,
Up to my true love and the dance:
Sing O my love, O my love, my love, my love;
This have I done for my true love.

Then up to heaven I did ascend.
Where now I dwell in sure substance
On the right hand of God, that man
May come unto the general dance:
Sing O my love, O my love, my love, my love;
This have I done for my true love.

Introduction

Dancing has always played a part in most religions, including Christianity, but where the latter is concerned it seems to have been regarded with a degree of suspicion, so that at best it has been tolerated, at worst denounced. It is true that there is evidence of dance in the scriptures, and in more recent years there has been a revival of liturgical dance in the church, but it can scarcely be said to be appreciated as being central to its life, as music is, for example. One of the reasons why this may be so almost certainly arises from a profound mistrust in Western Christianity of the body, and all that is related to it: sexuality, enjoyment, freedom, and much more besides, so that it has been thought necessary to tame the body, to keep it under control. The consequence of this is that our experience, our awareness, our lives are imbalanced, and if we have ignored and excluded a part of ourselves then the truth must be that we are not fully alive.

Dancing is one way in which the body can be recognised and accepted as part of the mystery and the reality of our humanity. It would be wrong to presume, of course, that dancing is therefore hedonistic and indulgent. Like many other things there is an element of training and discipline involved if the body is to be integrated rather than to dictate, dominate, and lead to dissolution. Balance is of the essence.

This book is not about dancing in that sense. Rather it begins with the image of dancing as conveying something of our experience of the mystery of life in Christ, for dance, above all, seems to have something to do with being fully alive, with spontaneity and freedom, as well as with discipline and control. It is, therefore, an image of wholeness, and of the fullness of life, and it is this to which we are called in Christ.

The words of *My Dancing Day* have long been significant for me. They are inescapably associated with the music to which the first four verses have been set by John Gardner, and are sung by many choirs as a carol at Christmas.[1] To my mind the music combines just that quality of life and abandonment, together with discipline and control, that characterises dance. This is achieved largely through the use of syncopated rhythms, so that within a controlled and stable framework of expectation there arises a sense of spontaneity, of freedom, with just the slightest hint (but no more!) of that kind of anarchy, which is necessary in all our experience if we are to be delivered from the dead hand of the letter into the freedom of the Spirit and the fullness of life. John Gardner's music encapsulates perfectly for me that sense of wholeness, exhilaration and life that I associate with dance. For that reason alone it is an image of our life in Christ.

The nature of dance itself, though, seems to me to offer an important insight into the way in which we experience, grow and reflect upon our life in Christ. As is the case in many other western art forms, the notion of development and progression plays a part in dance. In much ballet, for example, a story is the framework for dance, so that by means of dance we are involved in a narrative in which characters are introduced at the beginning, and the development of whose relationships leads to the resolution or otherwise at the end. There is a sense of linear progression from one thing to another, and this is central to our experience of life as a whole. From birth to death we have a sense that something is to happen in-between: we do not expect to be the same at the end as at the beginning. There is to be growth and development.

Dance is not all like that, though. In its most original forms dancing is rather more cyclical in character; it does not necessarily progress from one situation to another, rather it goes around in circles, almost literally! In the courtly dances out of which classical ballet grew, and in much social dancing today, the cyclical nature of the dance is more prominent than the developmental. It is true, of course, that dance provides ways of social interaction, and so in cyclical dances there may be all kinds of hidden developments taking place, but that does not deny the intrinsically cyclical nature of some dancing.

The awareness of these two essential characteristics of dance seems to me to be important, for to be aware of only one or the other results in imbalance and disorder. This is true of the way in which we experience reality, and of our life in Christ. Western culture tends to emphasise the more linear nature of experience. We prize logical thought and progress, for example, very highly, and this has been central to Christian experience, too. Eastern culture experiences life much more in terms of its cyclical character. The rising of the sun and its setting, for example, are the pivotal moments in the day, around which waking and sleeping, working and playing revolve. This may seem so obvious as to be hardly worth mentioning, but the plain fact of the matter is that in the west we are far less likely to be sensitive to the cyclical experience of reality, indeed there is almost certainly a profound mistrust and fear of it and for precisely the same reason that the body is regarded with suspicion. The body, in particular its involvement in the expression of our sexuality, threatens to overwhelm us with uncontrollable urges, and we perceive the lack of control to lead back to that chaos out of which God is creating order. Our predominant attitude to the body, then, is one of forcing its submission, rather than embracing it as a part of what it means to be human.

The body, of course, has its cycles, of which women are much more likely to be aware than men and that points to another reason why the body and the awareness of the cyclical nature of reality is less welcomed and appreciated in Western culture, for this awareness is much more associated with the feminine than the masculine, and the masculine view of reality has prevailed in the West. Along with the feminine awareness of cycles goes a much greater sensitivity towards the natural world, with the recurring cycles of the seasons and so on. Perhaps it is not surprising that, in the West at least, dancing has been considered to be an activity mainly for women, and where men have been dancers they have often been looked down upon.

Dancing, then, provides us with an image of wholeness, with a means of embracing opposites and holding them together in the hope of discovering wholeness, even when to do so seems to be difficult and painful, even impossible. Our life in Christ is about wholeness and reconciliation, about fullness and union, and if the linear and cyclical characteristics of dance provide us with an image of life in Christ, it is true, also, that our experience of Christ has both linear and cyclical qualities, and this influences the approach of this book; indeed one of the purposes is to be open to two ways of experiencing and reflecting upon the mystery of our life in Christ.

The words of *My Dancing Day* shape the framework of the meditations which follow, with each succeeding verse providing inspiration for the sequence of chapters. The poem progresses through the life of Christ from birth to ascension, and is thus thoroughly linear in its character. This arises not least from the central experience of Christianity, which is the grounding of our awareness of God in and through history. The historical life of Jesus is central to our relationship with God. Much of the reflection on our Christian faith and experience is governed by this sequential approach, so that in our theology we divide up matters of faith into neat categories, which has the advantage of making the exercise manageable, but the very order and control of which more often than not keeps the presence and the mystery of God at arm's length.

More importantly, though, is it so, that even if we accept the historicality of our faith and necessarily its revelation in time, and therefore its linear character, we do not experience it wholly in that way. Our experience of Christ has a cyclical character, too, and this is recognised, at least unconsciously, by the ordering of the liturgical year. Year in and year out we enter more deeply into the mystery of Christ made known in linear time in a cyclical manner. Throughout the world time is punctuated not only by the recurring seasons but also by the mysteries of Christ: Christmas, Easter, Pentecost and so on. This corresponds to our experience of Christ as much as, perhaps more than, does the sense that our growth in him is wholly logical and systematic. The awakening, for example, of the awareness of the reality of Christ differs from one person to another. For one it may arise out of the mystery of creativity and birth; for another out of suffering and loss. At some stage, though, we begin to discover that such things are not disconnected or unrelated, but rather that they belong together: there can be creativity in suffering, just as there can be birth in loss. Our participation in the life of Christ then is neither wholly linear nor wholly cyclical. Perhaps it pertains more to the nature of a spiral in which we experience the same thing over and over again in a slightly different way and at a deeper level.

These meditations, then, are based upon a poem that moves in linear progression, but which seek not to be confined by the dictates of logical thought alone. Instead there is a deliberate acceptance of the fact that themes recur and weave in and out of each other, but that as they do we do not return to precisely from where we started. If a necessary feature of dance is movement, then these meditations may be likened in part to the experience of viewing a sculpture: we have to begin somewhere, but we do not see it whole. As we walk around it so we begin to see it for what it is. It may be that it is only when we have viewed it from all angles that we can return to our initial vantage point with a sense of what to look for and how to look; and with that awareness we see the same thing differently.

Most importantly of all, however, dancing, of its very nature, invites involvement and participation. As an image of the mystery of life in Christ it suggests the centrality of experience: we are to know the reality of God for ourselves, and to live that reality from the inside.

Above all else, then, it is hoped that these meditations will enable the reader to be drawn more deeply into the mystery of Christ, for it is in Christ himself that God invites the whole of creation to dance in his love and to enter into the fullness and the joy of life.

CHAPTER ONE

Seeing

Tomorrow shall be my dancing day:
I would my true love did so chance
To see the legend of my play,
To call my true love to my dance:
Sing O my love, O my love, my love, my love;
This have I done for my true love.

One of my most treasured possessions is an oil painting which was left to me in the will of an elderly woman for whom I cared when I was first ordained. It hung just behind the door in the small room where she lived so that it was not immediately visible on entering. I had been asked to visit her because she was becoming progressively less well as a result of a stomach cancer.

From the very first moment that I saw the painting I was deeply moved by it, and its owner at the time noticed my reaction. I had not the slightest doubt that it was an exceptionally powerful work of art, and this delighted her, because that was not how it was universally appreciated by any means. Indeed to this day, where it hangs in our vicarage, by far the most common response to it is that people are glad that it hangs in our sitting room and not theirs!

Its original owner had been brought up as an Austrian Jew, but having fled from the Nazis to England during the Second World War she had embraced Christianity, and embarked upon a career as a highly respected psychotherapist. The artist in question had become her ward of court, and much love and affection was shared between them. In addition they shared a common bond through suffering:

she through her family's fate at the hands of the Nazis; he on account of periods of depression which he had to bear.

The painting which so struck me was conceived and executed during one of its creator's bleakest periods of almost suicidal depression, and it is not difficult to see that the painting itself reveals characteristics of that awful state. Its colours are overwhelmingly dark, mainly greys and black, with just a hint of red towards the bottom, which is visible when viewed from close range. This accounts, of course, for the predominantly negative reactions to it. To many it seems disturbing and menacing, too. That is not how I saw it from the first, nor do I see it so to this day. In the face I see pain and suffering which has been accepted and taken into itself in love. The deeply-set eyes exude compassion and understanding, and the whole bearing is one of dignity and the complete absence of any desire to retaliate.

People see it differently, and responses vary. One thing is abundantly clear to all, though. Not one person ever needs to ask who the subject is, for although it has a title it is obvious that the painting can be only one thing: the Head of Christ.

The varying responses to that painting illustrate the richness and the subtlety involved in what and how we see. At its most basic level what we mean by seeing is what we perceive with our eyes: light, colour, objects and so on. Thus in the painting what one person notices is the colour; another that the subject of the painting is a human head. Beyond that, though, no response is wholly neutral, for all have an awareness that something lies behind the painting itself. The reactions to the dark colours are not simply sensory: an awareness that they are dark. The colours, and how they are seen, awaken an emotional response. Further still the painting has the capacity to communicate meaning and value, an awareness, for example, of the horror of suffering, or of the love and compassion that may be drawn out from within it.

Seeing is not only a physical sensation. It has to do with making sense of what we see and how we see. It involves understanding, interpreting, valuing, judging, appreciating and much more. The interesting question about the painting, of course, is why the artist should have painted it in the first place. Most probably there was an inner creative urge which had to be obeyed, but why should it have been expressed thus? Presumably the act of painting was therapeutic, at least in part, but then why was it not a self-portrait? What did the artist see and invite us to see in his creation? Must it not have had something to do with the fact that in the depths of depression he wanted to see signs of hope and, at the very least, saw in Christ a companion in suffering, one who knew, understood and saw what was involved in his own darkness? Artists generally paint for others to see, too; even more so they invite us to see what and how they see, and in so doing enable us to see things differently. Why, after all, should it have been that the artist's guardian and I were so profoundly moved by the painting, whereas some others are not? I am sure that the answer lies in our own experience and awareness of suffering, so that we see in the painting something of ourselves, something of the artist, and most importantly of all for us, that we see all that illuminated by the suffering of Christ. That is not to say, though, that only one who shares the Christian faith is capable of perceiving it in that way. It is perfectly possible that someone quite hostile to Christianity might see in the painting something of the depths of Christ's suffering, and by means of that painting, see something of his significance, reality, mystery and love almost for the first time, and in that moment of perception discover that they see everything in a totally different light.

What we see is affected by how we see, and how we see is affected by what we see. Our seeing is shaped by the sum total of our experience, which begins at the moment of birth, and is being shaped at every moment. Initially our family circumstances influence us. If our most basic needs as a baby, for example, are met with love and care we come to perceive the world as being favourably disposed towards us, and we enter freely into a relationship with it. If the reverse is our experience then we grow up with a sense that the world is hostile, and, to an extent, we become enclosed within ourselves, hanging on to whatever security we think we may have. So, too, do cultural factors have a significant effect. Our schooling and education shape us in this way and that, so that we may come to see that academic excellence is of more importance than anything else, for instance, or that what matters is being happy, or that serving others is more honourable. This is not to suggest that any of these things are mutually exclusive; it is simply to say that we are taught to see in all kinds of ways. Very often a person, a group of people, a place, an environment or a particular experience have a signal effect on us, which changes our way of seeing or confirms it. All of us grow up in a tradition of one kind or another, which passes on to us and through us how and what to see. Individually and corporately we add to that tradition, by contributing to it our own experience, our own way of seeing. As a result a dialogue is set up by which we are mutually enriched, influenced, guided and corrected.

Generally speaking I consider myself to have been fairly fortunate in my overall life experience. My parents have been loving and generous, indeed self-sacrificing in the interest of their three children. I am not blind to their failings and I know that I share some of them, and have others of my own. My schooling and education were, in the main, happy and fulfilling. Not only is my cultural background Christian; my family and school environments instilled the practice of faith, for which I have always been grateful, in fact it was at school that I first sensed that I was being called to be a priest. It was while at university that I met and fell in love with the person whom I would marry and with whom I would help to nurture four children. To the surprise of many of my clerical friends, I thoroughly enjoyed my time at theological college, and have been blessed by the people and places where I have served as a priest. There have been, of course, negative and difficult experiences, too, the most decisive of which was the expectation for most of my formative years until near adulthood that together with my mother, brother and sister I would succumb to an hereditary disease. It was not until I was eighteen years of age that I discovered that this could not be so, and only in the not so distant past that, as a result of an illness, I came to terms with the legacy of anxiety stemming from childhood. I am aware that the expectation of an hereditary illness coloured the way my family saw things and influenced my perception of life. Not least I know that it was as a result of this experience that I grew up with a crippling anxiety about death, a fear of dying young, so that I pushed myself hard to achieve before it was too late, together with a horror of any kind of serious illness or failure. All of these things cast a serious slur on my general perception that life was good and that God was favourably disposed towards me.

In truth, my life experience is probably fairly unexceptional, and I recognise that the way I see things has been shaped and influenced by many factors. Little by little certain things have happened that have enabled trust to take precedence over the fear of loss. One experience stands out above all else, though, for it has coloured my perception of reality, and occurred when I was seventeen years of age. I was travelling in an underground train in London at rush hour. The train was packed to overflowing with people on their way home from work. What appeared to my eyes was a collection of individuals, scarcely with any identity at all. The clothes they wore, the briefcases they carried, the newspapers they read all contrived to lessen any sense of personal identity. What I saw was a mass of anonymous objects, all apparently encased and enclosed in their own isolation and separateness, relieved not even by the hint of conversation. There seemed to be a deliberate intention that no one person should impinge upon another, that there should be no flow of movement from one to another. In this awareness I was no less a separate entity than anyone else.

Quite without warning I was taken out of myself and transported by the experience of a love in which everyone in the compartment, myself included, was held, and which gave to each a real and unique personal identity. No longer were they faceless individuals. Rather at the deepest level of all they were seen to be part of one another, loved, and of infinite value and significance. In my mind's eye I saw each person going home, to be met and welcomed by people to whom he or she mattered. I saw an endless variety of persons in their unique individualities and yet bound together in a fundamental unity from beyond.

The description of the experience would seem to suggest that it lasted some time. In fact it was over in an instant, it had lasted no longer than it takes to blink an eye. So significant and powerful was it, though, that I can remember it vividly to this day. My way of seeing, my perception, my awareness was totally transformed, and yet the circumstances were overwhelmingly ordinary. It seemed to me then, and it still seems to me to this day, that I was the recipient of a gift of seeing things as they really are, an awareness of all things and all people grounded in the love of God.

That experience has been one of the touchstones of my life, and it is from within the context of the Christian tradition that I have sought to interpret, to understand, to see it. That tradition seeks to enable us to see our lives and experience as being grounded in God and his love, to perceive that there is meaning, value and purpose in the world, and that the clue to our ultimate fulfilment and happiness lies in acknowledging and living in the awareness of our fundamental relationship in and with God.

The tradition of faith, however, does not provide ready made answers as if to be used in an examination. Our seeing is far more than an intellectual exercise; it involves the whole person. Seeing is a product of our total experience. Thus the process of interpreting my youthful experience is one which continues. There have been times when my original way of seeing it has been challenged, and other times when it has been more than confirmed. Its confirmation, though, lies in its relation to another experience on the other side of the coin, as it were.

There is a place in Wales to which I have been on holiday with my family for some years now. To go there is like going home, not so much because things can be taken for granted, but rather because we feel at ease with ourselves, with each other, with the world and with God. Very quickly, if we allow ourselves to, we enter into the joy, the delight, the sheer pleasure simply of being.

One place especially has a kind of sacramental quality about it, that is to say it is itself a kind of doorway through which we pass into this depth of life. Above the Mawddach Estuary, tucked just below Cader Idris, are some lakes known as Cregennan. From the road beneath there is a signpost. There is no indication whatsoever, though, of what beauty lies concealed just below the mountains. For that reason our initial stumbling across it, seemingly by chance, had about it a quality of grace, the unexpectedness of pure gift. As the winding road levelled out we seemed to be drawn out of ourselves by a presence wholly beyond us and yet most tenderly embracing.

Now, after several years, familiarity has not dulled my response. The senses are still heightened to a new intensity. It feels as if one is being opened up in body, mind and spirit, indeed truly being brought to life. Above all, though, as life flows in, the all-encompassing awareness is of a depth of silence, which is paradoxically deafening in its magnitude; not an empty silence, but one which is filled with presence. Such silence awakens within me once again an awareness of the depths of my own being, far beyond the physical senses, and yet which hints at an even greater fullness into which to be drawn. Between the silence of Cregennan and the silence of my own being there is a hidden communication, the consciousness of a relationship in which all things are held together in unity and love. I feel integrated and at peace.

It has not always been like that. I remember a holiday in the same place some years ago in which there was only a sense of fragmentation. I felt alienated from my surroundings, from nature, from my family, and from what I understood to be God. I was completely enclosed within myself and there was no joy, no delight, no spontaneity, no sense of the thrill at being alive. In fact the reverse was the case. At the time I could not have articulated it thus but I was actually burdened with the sense of my own existence, or, more precisely, with the awareness of my self-enclosed, isolated existence. Desperately I searched for a way out of this inner prison, which was none other than hell, but my own efforts were of no avail, indeed they made matters worse. I became unbearable to myself and to my family. Frantically I tried to pull myself out by rationalising, by seeking to persuade myself logically that I was not seeing into the heart of reality and discovering it to be totally devoid of any meaning or purpose, or grounding in a reality beyond itself, but the more I did so the worse I became. I found myself plummeting in an ever deepening spiral of despair, doubt and anxiety. I held on for all I was worth to anything that gave me a grip on what I saw as reality, for I feared that to do otherwise would lead me into an eternally separated existence, the merest hint of which seemed intolerable.

It was only when I was physically, emotionally, mentally and spiritually exhausted by this whole experience that the struggle ended, and paradoxically it was not by continuing to hang on but by letting go, even, as it seemed at the time, at the risk of disappearing into oblivion. What was called for was an act of surrender, in the sense of an act of trust, and in making that surrender I relinquished the sense of my separate existence and was met by a reality beyond, in whose being my own was held: God. In that moment of letting go came the restoration of peace and equilibrium.

These two poles of experience, of the union of all things in God on the one hand, and of the emptiness and meaningless of existence not grounded in anything beyond itself, have influenced the way I see perhaps more than anything else. The question which may well be asked is this: which of the two is the way of seeing more in line with the way things are? The answer is both. I have come to see that reality ungrounded in God is indeed empty and meaningless, and that only when reality is grounded in God are things most truly themselves. Or perhaps it should be put differently: everything is grounded in God; it is our failure to see that which leads to the sense of our separate existence, to alienation and fragmentation and to all that follows from it. Our way of seeing is in need of education and restoration. Wherein lies the cause of our faulty perception, and how is our true perception to be restored?

It is here that the Scriptures come into their own, for their purpose is indeed to open our eyes to the reality of God. At the beginning of the Book of Genesis, in the third chapter, the very concern with seeing is addressed. In the same way that an artist paints a picture and invites us to see things as he or she does, so does the story of the Fall paint a picture in words. By means of myth and symbol an awareness of our life in relation to God is mediated. By entering into the story, by seeing through the eyes of the story, we begin to see with the awareness which the story itself seeks to convey. By means of the story the same awareness is evoked in us as inspired the story itself. The whole purpose of the story is to show that our seeing, our perception, is the clue to living in harmony with God and everything else, or not.

Of central interest is the tree. The man and the woman

have been created by God and put in the garden of Eden. They are told by God:

'You may freely eat of every tree of the garden; but of the tree of the knowledge of good and evil you shall not eat, for in the day that you eat of it you shall die.'[1]

The attraction of the tree, however, is too great and the woman is persuaded by the words of the serpent:

' "You will not die; for God knows that when you eat of it your eyes will be opened, and you will be like God, knowing good and evil."

So when the woman saw that the tree was good for food, and that it was a delight to the eyes, and that the tree was to be desired to make one wise, she took of its fruit and ate; and she also gave some to her husband, who was with her, and he ate. Then the eyes of both were opened, and they knew that they were naked; and they sewed fig leaves together and made loincloths for themselves.

They heard the sound of the Lord God walking in the garden at the time of the evening breeze, and the man and his wife hid themselves from the presence of the Lord God among the trees of the garden.'[2]

Like any other myth this is rich in symbol and layers of meaning. It should be remembered that its purpose is indeed to suggest, to evoke and convey the awareness that lies behind it. Initially there is something perplexing about the command not to eat the fruit of the tree simply because the act of eating will lead to the knowledge of good and evil. What is wrong, after all, with being aware of good and evil? Behind this lies the awareness that in the emergence out of an undifferentiated consciousness to a consciousness of distinction and differentiation, and thus to self-awareness, which is a necessary process in the growth towards the fullness of life, there is also a danger, and the conscious refusal to be aware of good and evil is where our problems begin.

Thus the paradox lies in the fact that in the opening of

the eyes to reality there is a simultaneous blinding, an inability to see whole. The significance of eating the fruit resides in the presumption of the man and the woman that they can do whatever they like without reference to God. By putting themselves in the place of God they do not in fact become like him; rather they usurp his position, and exclude him from their view of reality, and in the process lose their vision of the whole. In essence what they do is to put themselves in the centre of the picture, and their awareness becomes restricted to what can be seen when they believe that they are the ultimate referents of truth and reality. From this partial and unbalanced vision the world disintegrates into fragmentation and division. Not only is the sense of the unity of all things in God lost; God himself is excluded.

The truth mediated by this myth corresponds to my experience. The temptation always is to limit vision to what is available to the senses, to believe that all that exists has no ground in a reality beyond ourselves. The wisdom of every spiritual tradition encourages us to see that all our problems and difficulties lie in the desire to see ourselves as the centre of reality. In order to see correctly we have to let go of self and die to self-centredness and allow a larger vision, a more whole awareness to take its place.

How do we do this? Here again we stumble across another paradox, for if our problems arise from opening our eyes to one part of reality and shutting them to the far greater part, then restoration comes when we do the reverse: we shut our eyes to partial reality, which sometimes, even often, seems like shutting our eyes to everything we know, and allow ourselves to see in the dimension of a greater reality. This is none other than the way of faith, which is the opening up to an intuitive awareness of God, beyond that which we can ordinarily see. The author of the Letter to the Hebrews expresses it as follows:

'Now faith is the assurance of things hoped for, the

conviction of things not seen. By faith we understand that the worlds were prepared by the word of God, so that what is seen was made from things that are not visible.'[3]

The way of faith is the surrender and commitment of one's whole being in trust and love away from what is known, which is always limited and partial, to what as yet remains unknown or only dimly perceived, but whole. By faith our capacity for the direct intuitive knowledge of God is unlocked. With the inner eye of faith and love we begin to see what is unseen by not seeing, to know what is unknown by not knowing.

In many instances such an awakening seems almost to be forced upon us: a bereavement, an illness, a disappointment or a disaster, which deprives of all that was of value, and of the very basis on which life had been built. Some become embittered by such experiences and turn in on themselves. Others, however, find themselves looking beyond, or even entering immediately into an awareness that there is more to life than they thought. So, too, can we be taken out of ourselves unexpectedly by the love of another, by the beauty of a work of art or nature. Again in such experiences we are awakened to a reality beyond our limited selves. In that awakening there seems to be an invitation to let go, to surrender, and in letting go to discover that we find all, as well as an implicit promise that if we relinquish ourselves we shall indeed find ourselves.

That invitation and promise is focused above all in Jesus. He invites us to see from his perspective by committing ourselves wholly to him. To follow him is to have our way of seeing shaped by his, to enter into his perception and awareness. To see with Jesus' eyes involves living in his way, which is above all a letting go into the relationship with the Father. There are no shortcuts, however. His way is a way of dying to self, and discovering such dying as the only means to life. That is why his way of seeing is not merely intellectual assent, for we can only enter into his awareness, his way of seeing, if we too are prepared to let go of everything. For that reason his conversation with two of John the Baptist's disciples is tantalisingly open-ended:

'When Jesus turned and saw them following, he said to them, "What are you looking for?" They said to him, "Rabbi" (which translated means Teacher), "where are you staying?" He said to them, "Come and see".'[4]

The response to Jesus' question made by the two disciples betrays an embarrassment, a failure of nerve: they were surely not following him just to discover where he was staying! They had been pointed in the direction of Jesus by John the Baptist who had said: ' "Look, here is the Lamb of God".'[5] The disciples were in some way attracted to Jesus, really wanting to see who Jesus was, but the only path to discovery lies in the commitment of the self in faith and trust: 'Come and see'. The underlying purpose of St. John's Gospel is to enable us to see Jesus, and in showing his way of seeing to encourage the loss of ourselves in order to receive the life of God through him:

'No one has ever *seen* God. It is God the only Son, who is close to the Father's heart, who has made him known'.[6] 'Whoever has *seen* me has seen the Father.'[7] 'We have *seen* the Lord.'[8] 'And the Word became flesh and lived among us, and we have seen his glory, the glory as of a father's only son, full of grace and truth.'[9]

When we allow our seeing to be informed by Jesus himself we enter into a quite different dimension of reality. If we are prepared voluntarily to undergo the loss of self and be drawn into his way of seeing we enter into the relationship he shares with his Father in the Spirit. We begin to perceive that everything is grounded in the mysterious love of God, a giving and receiving of love in perfect unity. In Jesus God seeks to catch our eye, to 'see the legend of his play', as the carol suggests. More than that though. As we see that play we perceive that God calls us his 'true love', to let go of everything, to lose self, and abandon ourselves to the exhilaration of the dance. In so doing God invites us to do no less than to participate in his own being, the divine dance of love, so that in and through Christ he might dance his love in us.

CHAPTER TWO

Enfleshing

Then was I born of a virgin pure,
Of her I took fleshly substance;
Thus was I knit to man's nature,
To call my true love to my dance:
Sing O my love, O my love, my love, my love;
This have I done for my true love.

It has been my immensely good fortune to grow up in a musical family. My maternal grandmother played the piano and the mandolin by ear and in consequence was the life and soul of many a party. My mother herself learnt the piano and my father has always enjoyed singing. It is scarcely surprising that with such a background I should have inherited musical gifts, together with my brother and sister, and those gifts have subsequently been passed on to my own children.

From an early age I was eager to play the piano, and before I had any real idea of what to do I would go and 'tootle'. At the age of seven I was allowed to start taking proper lessons and I made quick progress. In the course of time I developed an interest in composition and conducting, and entertained the fairly idiotic idea that I might be able to pursue a career as a composer or a conductor. It was a vain notion because deep in my bones I knew that I was not in that kind of league.

The composition and performance of music reveals a great deal about who we are. A composer seeks to communicate something of himself or herself in music. What is seeking to be communicated will vary from one composer to another, but the notes on the score and their subsequent performance seek to embody, to enflesh the composer's inner intentions and ideas. In the process of composition, as a result of seeking to give form to musical ideas, the composer is drawn into a deeper self knowledge and awareness. It will be discovered, for example, whether the music is an authentic expression of what he or she wishes to communicate. From the music will be reflected an awareness of the composer's concerns, intentions and ideas. Motives for composing will be revealed, and by means of this whole experience he or she will, in a very real sense, come to know himself or herself in and through the music.

My own experience of composition was often a painful one. In my younger years my main concern seemed to be to write something avant-garde, and so I attempted to compose all kinds of weird and wonderful music. In the depths of my being, however, I knew that what was being written was inauthentic and shallow because I was not being true to myself. More often than not I sought to compose with my head alone so that the music seemed to be devoid of inner spirit. With time I learnt to let go of my head and write from my depths, and very occasionally I still have the opportunity to do so. Nobody, least of all I, would claim that the music is of any significance; except that its worth is immeasurably greater as a genuine expression of me, than something which was technically brilliant but no more than that.

The sole object of a performer is to let someone else's music come to life through oneself. It might be thought that all that is required is to play or sing the notes accurately, observing the composer's dynamic markings and general directions in such a way that the composer's intentions are expressed; but it is rather more subtle than that. Truly to express the composer's intentions requires the absence of all self-interest on the part of the performer. There has to be a willingness to lose oneself in order to be brought to life in the music. The relationship between composer and performer in the music is indeed one of love in mutual openness – there is a giving and receiving from one to the other. All the gifts of technique and interpretation are to be placed at the service of the composer's music, but sometimes, even with some professional musicians, it seems to be the other way round: the music is treated as nothing more than the vehicle for the performer's self-glorification. On the occasions of such a performance a sense of prostitution can be detected. By contrast when the performer is completely empty of self-interest and self-seeking the composer's original intentions are realised so that in the very process the performer is raised to a new awareness, and precisely because of the absence of self-centredness, is in fact expressive of his or her true self in relation to the composer and the composer's music.

Our awareness of the nature and purpose of life itself is very much like that of a composer, and of a performer in relation to a composer: creation, ourselves included, is to express the mind, the purpose, the intention of God, and creation is only truly itself when it does that. In responding to the fact of our existence we are faced with a fundamental choice: either to place everything and everyone at our own disposal so that our overriding concern is to tailor life to suit our own intentions and purposes; or to place ourselves in the service of God, to be the embodiment, the expression of his will. More than that, though: by enfleshing the will of God we actually participate in his life and being, as a performer does in the realisation of a composer's intentions.

We are not so accustomed to thinking of ourselves as embodying the life of God, nor do we necessarily perceive ourselves as participating in God's life, letting him dance in us, and us in him. There are most probably two reasons for this: first the fear of identifying the world with God, so that there is no distinction between the two; alternatively the fear that the world itself is not real, that matter has no basis in reality, and is in fact to be left behind, discarded as being no more than a distraction. Our experience of God in Christ prohibits either view, because in him we perceive God to have become incarnate, enfleshed: he took 'fleshly substance' and was 'knit to man's nature'; and although Christ is in many ways different from us it is not he who is abnormal: he is what God intends humanity truly to be; it is we who are abnormal. What Christ reveals is no more than was there from the beginning.

The two creation stories at the beginning of Genesis seek to convey something of our awareness of having been created by God, intended to be expressive of his will, purpose and life. Their task is to mediate, in so far as this is possible, an intuitive awareness of the reality of God, and to evoke a response, and in so doing they are complementary. In the first[1] God brings all things into being with awesome power. He has only to speak and his inner intentions are given created form. Everything is perceived to proceed from the creative will of God: all that exists, from the most basic form of life to the human being. Finally the human being is created in God's own image as the pinnacle of creation.

There are two contrasting characteristics of the awareness of God here. The first is that God is utterly beyond us, transcendent. Our most basic experience in relation to God is that we are creatures, which is to say that we know that our own being is not self-devised: we are completely dependent for our own being upon God. It may seem rather obvious to suggest that one of the purposes of this story is to declare that we have been created by God, but it seeks to do more than simply communicate a proposition: it focuses our intuitive awareness that our whole being is grounded in a reality greater than our own, in God, in relation to whom alone we discover our own ultimate truth, identity and nature. In this respect we are utterly different from God: we may have powers of creativity but not of this nature. Creation points to a God of infinite resourcefulness and creativity, the awareness of which draws us into a sense of profound mystery. We marvel and wonder; we are aware of our own nothingness, which is not self-abasement, but a recognition that what we are, indeed, that we are at all, is a sheer gift. The Psalmist articulates such an awareness thus:

'When I look at your heavens, the work of your fingers, the moon and the stars that you have established; what are human beings that you are mindful of them, mortals that you care for them? Yet you have made them little lower than God, and crowned them with glory and honour.'[2]

The most natural response in this awareness of God is one of praise and adoration. God does not demand this of us; it is the natural movement of our whole being; an expression of awe:

'Let them praise the name of the Lord, for his name alone is exalted; his glory is above earth and heaven.'[3]

The second characteristic of the awareness of God in this story contrasts to an extent with God's distance and otherness in the recognition that creation nevertheless is in some way or other expressive of God himself. God is portrayed as speaking:

'Then God said, "Let there be light"; and there was light.'[4]

The temptation to envisage God anthropomorphically has to be resisted: that is partly what the story is seeking to convey, that God is different. At the same time, though, the image of speech points to God's self-communication and self-expression. We use words to communicate our inmost thoughts and intentions. So God's word is a symbol of the awareness that God expresses himself in what he creates, and supremely in human beings who bear his image. Thus it is that alongside our basic awareness of God's otherness and our nothingness goes a corresponding awareness that at the same time creation is expressive of God, and that human beings are like him, to the extent that in some measure we share God's own nature. When we look at ourselves we see a reflection of God.

The second of the two stories[5] also seeks to mediate the awareness of our having been created by God and conveys the sense of a relationship between human beings and God of the utmost intimacy. Creation is completely dependent upon God for its being, but the story characterises our awareness that in some mysterious way we share in God's own life. This is done by the image of breath:

'Then the Lord God formed man from the dust of the ground, and breathed into his nostrils the breath of life; and man became a living being.'[6]

The communication of breath from one to another is a most intimate act. The attempt by one human being, for example, to bring back to life another who has ceased to be by mouth to mouth resuscitation, involves intimate physical contact, and into one who is dead is passed the very life force of the other, so that the restoration to life involves a participation, a sharing, in the life of the other. Breathing is profoundly mysterious, and in all religions the attentive awareness of the breath is known to lead to the intuitive awareness of God, of the source of all life, who is beyond all living things and yet present in them, too. In the Hebrew awareness of God, physical breath, the natural life-force, is seen to proceed from God's own life, such that in Hebrew the words wind, breath and spirit are almost interchangeable, as can be gleaned from Psalm 104, itself a hymn of praise to God the creator:

'When you take away their breath (Hebrew: Ruach) they die and return to their dust. When you send forth your spirit (Hebrew: Ruach), they are created; and you renew the face of the ground.'[7]

If we allow ourselves to be drawn into the awareness that these two stories seek to mediate we find ourselves on the brink of a staggering mystery. All that exists communicates and is expressive of the mind, the intention, the will, the purpose of God, and as we look into ourselves we see

God reflected. Creation comes into being in and through God's Word. So, too, does it participate in God's own life by means of God's Spirit, which enlivens all that comes to be in the Word. The Spirit breathes in everything, enabling it truly to be a living expression of the Eternal Word of God. So close to God are we, so identified are we with him, that it is scarcely surprising that we struggle to see him. We live in him and he in us in the most intimate way imaginable as St. Paul himself knew:

'The God who made the world and everything in it, he who is Lord of heaven and earth, does not live in shrines made by human hands, nor is he served by human hands, as though he needed anything, since he himself gives to all mortals life and breath and all things. From one ancestor he made all nations to inhabit the whole earth, and he allotted the times of their existence and the boundaries of the places where they would live, so that they would search for God and perhaps grope for him and find him – though indeed he is not far from each one of us. For "in him we live and move and have our being"; as even some of your own poets have said, "For we too are his offspring".'[8]

The notion that human beings, with the whole of creation, should in some way be an embodiment, an enfleshing of the life of God is far from being eccentric: it is at the very heart of Christian faith and experience. Yet we are aware that it is not quite so, that in some measure we fail to embody the life of God as he intends us to. The reason lies in our abuse of the freedom God has given us. Just as a musical performer is free to make an act of self-surrender and self-offering in the service of the composer for the realisation of the composer's creative expression of his or her inner conception, or not, as the case may be, so we have the same freedom in relation to God: to give ourselves freely and willingly to God so that he can realise his purpose and express his life in us, or to appropriate to ourselves all that he has created as the means of our self-expression unrelated to God. It is a bitter irony to discover that here is the truth from which human beings constantly run: that the path of self-centredness and self-seeking leads to the loss of our true selves, and that the path to the fullness of life lies in letting go of ourselves, of life itself, in order that we may live God's life in us and so truly be what God intends. Sin is no more and no less than the refusal to let go of self and allow God to enflesh his life in us. We can often see the truth so easily and yet we find it so difficult to live it. Our aspirations are one thing, our realisations quite another. The words of St. Paul illuminate our condition perfectly:

'I do not do the good I want, but the evil I do not want is what I do. Now if I do what I do not want, it is no longer I that do it, but sin that dwells within me. So I find it to be a law that when I want to do what is good, evil lies close at hand. For I delight in the law of God in my inmost self, but I see in my members another law at war with the law of my mind, making me captive to the law of sin that dwells in my members. Wretched man that I am! Who will rescue me from this body of death?'[9]

The answer which St Paul gives from his profoundest experience is this: Jesus Christ.

The uniting of God and humanity in Christ is a profound mystery and the knowledge of just who he is comes not from intellectual speculation or a process of reasoning but from experience. In one sense it appears that he can be understood as the natural outcome of the creative process. As a human being he lives as he is intended to, open to the Spirit, and in such a way that the image of God is brought to life in him. He reveals what true humanity is like. In this sense we perceive in him an image of ourselves. It is impossible, however, for us to be content with a view that explains Christ as a natural development. Experience demands that we say more, however difficult it may be to express it. Unlike us, Jesus reveals no evidence of sinfulness, which is to say that he was wholly given to God in such a way that God's own life lived in and through him. At this level it can be seen that he showed us how to live, supremely in his dying, for by refusing to cling to life or to anything for himself, he allowed God's life to flow in him. Even that, however, significant though it may be, does not account for our experience adequately, for our experience is that it is in and through him that life flows to us from God. So it is that after the resurrection, for example, he confers life on his disciples:

'Jesus said to them again, "Peace be with you. As the Father has sent me, so I send you." When he had said this, he breathed on them and said to them, "Receive the Holy Spirit".'[10]

The breath of life which is breathed into creation to give it life is that same breath of life, the Holy Spirit, which Jesus breathes onto his disciples after the resurrection. In and through Jesus something new and unexpected happens. We find ourselves being brought to life in him:

'If anyone is in Christ, there is a new creation: everything old has passed away; see, everything has become new! All this is from God, who reconciled us to himself through Christ.'[11]

All this is from God! That is what our experience of Christ tells us. Christ is not to be understood as the outcome of a natural human process alone, but rather as revealing God, and as coming from him. When we read in the Letter to the Colossians that:

'He is the image of the invisible God, the firstborn of all creation; for in him all things in heaven and on earth were created things visible and invisible, whether thrones or dominions or rulers or powers – all things have been created through him and for him. He himself is before all things, and in him all things hold together',[12]

or in St John's Gospel that:

'In the beginning was the Word, and the Word was with God, and the Word was God. He was in the beginning with God. All things came into being through him, and without him not one thing came into being. What has come into being in him was life, and the life was the light of all people ... And the Word became flesh and lived among us, and we have seen his glory, the glory as of a father's only son, full of grace and truth',[13] we are being encouraged to see that in Christ we glimpse not just the image of humanity but the image of *God*. It is almost impossible to express this adequately in words, but it means something like this: what we see in Christ is the form, the embodiment in a human life, of that which is eternally in God, and is God, in and through which God brings everything into being. In Christ we are given a revelation of God and of creation, which has been revealed supremely in and through him.

On the basis of this awareness and experience we are able to be much clearer about the nature of God, of creation, and of their relation to each other. God exists independently of creation, as the source of all that it is. There is also within him, independent of creation, a self-expression and self-communication: the Eternal Word. This Word is God, and is the way in which God knows himself. That which unites God as the source of life with his eternal self-communication is the Spirit.

Creation comes into being in and through the Eternal Word, so that it is distinct from God, and yet is a form of God's eternal self-expression. God and creation are not one, but neither are they two. Creation is united with God and shares in his life by means of the Spirit. It is in and through Christ that this is revealed.

It is possible to see then, from our experience of Christ that creation is not to be identified with God in such a way that there is no distinction, nor is it possible to claim that matter has no basis in reality. Rather is it the case that through Christ God is in all things and all things are in God. To come to this realisation by means of intuitive awareness is indeed a revelation. All things are then known in their relation to the Spirit. No longer is it possible to separate matter from Spirit where creation is concerned: there is no separate sacred sphere, for everything is holy, participating in the life of God. Nothing is outside God; all things are in him. The most menial tasks are then perceived to have as much to do with God as the most exalted. In this awareness there is a reverence for all created things, and this reverence is a consecration of all things in God. No longer is matter a barrier to God, or the body tiresome; everything dances and sings with God's life.

Such knowledge remains hidden from us in two ways, each resulting in imbalance and distortion. The first derives from perceiving the world as it is available to the senses to be all there is. When the awareness of the spiritual dimension of reality is excluded humanity gradually comes to be seen as the centre of everything. Creation in all its richness is reduced to whatever human beings choose it to be in the service of their own ends. Reverence disappears, and people and the things of the natural world become no more than objects. The delicately balanced inter-relationship which creation reveals is destroyed with devastating consequences. When the world is devoid of God we become dominated by a spirit of acquisition which deprives us of our freedom. The evidence of this is an enslavement to the things of the material world without relation to God. Having lost our freedom we forego the possibility of true happiness and fulfilment and search for them in things which are ultimately incapable of delivering them. The earth is plundered by the rich and powerful, leading the poor to greater poverty, and the rich to a sense of ever increasing emptiness when the deepest needs of the human spirit are ignored. The discomfort of alienation tries to find relief in the abuse of the body through sex, drugs, alcohol, and anything that can be consumed in larger quantities. The consequent breakdown in relationships on every scale is inevitable, and so the cycle of frustration and deprivation on every level is perpetuated.

It is scarcely surprising that for those who reach the conclusion that the world, when emptied of spiritual awareness, has all but lost hope, there should be little alternative than to seek refuge in a realm which purports to have little or nothing to do with the created order. The world is considered to be a distraction from the things which are ultimately important. The awareness of God is undoubtedly recovered, but what is lost in the process is the appreciation of a vast dimension of reality. The need to be free of all that hinders union with God, so it is thought, is expressed in a harshness of attitude to all that is not of God. The body with all its uncontrollable and perplexing urges has to be beaten into submission by the denials of the basic pleasures of eating, drinking and love-making. This attitude, however, reveals an attachment, a clinging to such things just as strong as in those for whom the material dimension of reality is considered to be all there is. Ultimately this engenders, or at least feeds, a competitive spirit, which expresses itself not only in relation to others, but more importantly perhaps, in relation to ourselves, for the more superficial part of us is locked in combat with the self through which the life of God flows, and which is grounded in him. The harshness and lack of compassion which is then directed towards ourselves is also directed towards others, and we become blinded to the presence of God in them and in all creation, unaware of the Spirit which flows in and through relationships with our neighbour, and the way in which the denial of the need to integrate and unite the material basis of reality with the spiritual actually interrupts the flow of the Spirit.

Neither of these two attitudes, either of attempting to evacuate material reality of its spiritual basis, or of seeking to find union with God by denying the significance of our embodied existence, corresponds with what God has revealed in Christ. In him God has become incarnate, enfleshed, in such a way that gives value to every aspect of our lives when received as coming from him. The resurrection and ascension of Christ confirms the value of creation and the environment in which we are drawn into union with God. The significance of the empty tomb, and the appearances of the Risen Christ in a spiritual body, lies in the fact that in the end the whole of creation, which in a real sense is Christ's body, is to be raised up and transformed into the fullness of life in God. As we let go of ourselves and open ourselves up to God here and now so the Spirit brings us to life in the Eternal Word and the work of resurrection already happens. In this work nothing is to be left out and everything has the capacity to contribute to the fullness of life in God:

'If anyone is in Christ, there is a new creation; everything old has passed away; see, everything has become new!'[14]

CHAPTER THREE

Consenting

In a manger laid and wrapped I was,
So very poor, this was my chance,
Betwixt an ox and a silly poor ass,
To call my true love to my dance;
Sing O my love, O my love, my love, my love;
This have I done for my true love.

Within the comparatively recent past it has become acceptable practice for fathers to be present at the births of their children should they so wish. It has been my very great joy to attend the birth of each of our four children. However much there may have been signs that the pregnancies had proceeded according to plan, the moment of birth on each occasion was the cause both of apprehension and of wonder. The emergence of life in a human baby is simply amazing.

When our first child was born I remember that as I took him into my hands for the first time I was also overcome by intense fear. This child had been in the womb for nine months, during which time the miraculous process of life had patiently and secretly brought him to the stage where he would be able to survive outside the womb, and he was being entrusted to me, vulnerable and helpless, for me to do with him exactly what I felt so minded to do. With awe I realised that his life was literally in my hands. It may seem strange to say that at that moment I could think of such a thing but I was almost unbearably conscious of the fact that his well-being depended entirely on my willingness to receive and hold that which had been entrusted to me. In a moment of seeming irrationality I became gripped

by the horror of dropping him. More than that I recognised that his being held securely in my arms depended not
only upon the avoidance of an untimely accident; it also
rested upon my consent, my free choice simply not to open
my arms and let him fall as a deliberate action. The sense
of responsibility of being entrusted with life was overwhelming, and I wondered and marvelled that God should
give us such freedom, and that so much should depend
upon what we do with it.

We do not expect to find the creator of the universe
lying 'so very poor, betwixt an ox and a silly poor ass'.
Our natural inclination would be to associate him with all
the trappings of the great in the eyes of the world, but the
very poverty and humility of the birth of Christ themselves
reveal the nature of God, for just as any child depends for
its survival or otherwise at the moment of birth upon the
attitudes and actions of others, so does God make himself
vulnerable to the freedom with which he has endowed his
creation. The birth of Christ was fragile, precariously
balanced upon all kinds of whims and consents: the
consent of his mother to his conception in the first place;
the consent of Joseph not to divorce his betrothed and
abandon his responsibility; the whim of the Emperor
Augustus, who, as Luke recounts, initiated a census, which
necessitated a precarious and tiring journey when Mary
was near to the completion of her term; the whim of King
Herod, who, Matthew tells us, demanded the slaughter of
all male children under two years of age, in order to ward
off what he perceived as a threat to himself and his
authority occasioned by the birth of Christ. Incredible
though it may seem all this is consistent with a God who
prizes freedom, and who consigns the realisation of his
purposes to that very creation which he has freely brought
into being, and which he has endowed with the freedom
which is itself a mark of his image with which it is
stamped.

The author of true freedom must of necessity conceal

himself, otherwise his visible presence would almost determine and demand a response, which would lessen the freedom and dignity of his creatures. God comes to be known as one who so entrusts himself into the hands of his creation that he allows himself to be excluded from it, banished to the margins, as the birth of Christ reveals, and as his death on a cross, brought about by the exercise of God-given human freedom, confirms. Paradoxically this is the character of true love, which so values and cherishes the beloved that it will allow the object of love the freedom to grow to true maturity through risk and failure, as well as through encouragement and sacrifice. Indeed God risks the fulfilment of his creative purposes on their almost inevitable and total failure, which is why victory and disaster combine on the cross. Love reveals its true colour in the desire and the willingness to risk everything for the sake of the beloved.

The outcome of God's creative purpose depends upon human consent, the consent to let God come out of hiding as it were, the consent which, out of love, returns the outcome of all things to the loving freedom of the creator. In this movement is seen the nature of love's consummation: in love God freely entrusts himself into the hands of his creation, and where the consent is given creation entrusts itself in a response of love to the rightful claim of God. In the mutual poverty of love there is union in the presence of the one to the other.

Consent is the key to the consummation of love, for only by consent can love be consciously fulfilled. Creation is itself endowed with love from the beginning. God pours himself out in love in the very act of creating. All things come into being in the Word and are enlivened by the Spirit, so the whole of creation is grounded in the love of God from the start. The conscious fulfilment of that love depends upon the willingness of creation freely to let itself belong to God as the place where his love holds sway, or to reject its divine grounding and turn its back on its very origins in the Word. It is to this awareness that the Prologue to St John's Gospel attests:

'He was in the world, and the world came into being through him; yet the world did not know him. He came to what was his own, and his own people did not accept him. But to all who received him, who believed in his name, he gave power to become children of God, who were born not of blood or of the will of the flesh or of the will of man, but of God.'[1]

The poverty of divine love, celebrated also by St Paul in his Letter to the Philippians[2], begins to realise its patient hope in the moment that we consent consciously and freely to God's entry into the depths of our being. Divine poverty is met with human poverty, the renunciation of a self-determined life, and by the action of the Spirit we are brought to birth in Christ, and he in us, so that in our poverty we might receive the riches of Christ:

'For you know the generous act of our Lord Jesus Christ, that though he was rich, yet for your sakes he became poor, so that by his poverty you might become rich'.[3]

We rarely appreciate the poverty of spirit required of us if God is truly to be allowed entry into our lives. We have only to think of his own condescension, and at the same time to recall that we are created in the image of a God who consents to such poverty himself, to realise that most of the time we have hardly begun truly to consent to our own poverty that we might be filled with God. If God is indeed to be all in all it means that there is to be no space, no point anywhere in creation, which is to remain outside the presence and love of God. This requires a consent that God should possess us at every level of our being, body, mind and spirit. Consent to the action of God is to be made at every moment and at every level. Reflection on our experience reveals that if we do consent it is almost as if it is on our terms rather than God's, and we know that in so many subtle and not-so-subtle ways we cling to our own supposed riches and fail to surrender ourselves in poverty to the love of God. Instead we seek to build ourselves up in our own strength, little realising that true strength, true wealth lies in the letting go of everything into the fullness of God, entrusting ourselves to him alone.

God's overwhelming desire is to give himself to us in love. For that to be possible we have to consent to our poverty, to our emptiness, to receive all that we are as a gift of God's love, to be welcomed in gratitude. Apart from God, and without him, we are indeed nothing; our being is utterly dependent upon him. Poverty, then, is the essential condition of our relationship with God, and is, paradoxically, the only means by which we enter into the fullness of life as Jesus' own words suggest:

'Enter through the narrow gate; for the gate is wide and the road is easy that leads to destruction, and there are many who take it. For the gate is narrow and the road is hard that leads to life, and there are few who find it.' [4]

It is possible for us to be aware of our poverty at every moment. Then do we receive everything as coming from God, indeed as bearing God, as a manifestation of God's presence by which he entrusts himself to us. We rarely have the humility required, though: the desire to be nothing in ourselves in order to be everything in God, so that more often than not the awareness of our true poverty is given to us as something painful and distressing. This awareness can arise in the most ordinary circumstances of life, and we awaken to it largely through failure, through the collapse of our own efforts and the dawning recognition of our own powerlessness.

Thus it is that the experiences from which we most earnestly wish to run away and hide are likely to be the very ones that can open us up to the presence of God if only we will allow them to. God seeks our consent to poverty in the most ordinary, basic occurrences of life, not to beat us into submission, but so that he might give himself to us in love. Such experiences are examples of the narrow gate to which Jesus refers, and they may come in any of a number of forms, such as illness, when we realise that we may no longer have any control over our own health, or the breakdown of a relationship, the failure of an ambition, the rejection of love, the loss of employment, the pain of misunderstanding, the death of a loved one: all these and many others are occasions when we are invited to become deeply aware of our own poverty.

It may seem strange to dwell upon such things, indeed there may be a suspicion that there is even something masochistic and distorted in deliberately drawing attention to them as the means by which God gives himself to us. Such a suspicion, however, arises from the refusal to accept and consent to the most radical awareness of our poverty of all: that God is God, that the world exists as he, in his wisdom, has created it and that we either accept it, and in so doing find that his love embraces all things in unity, despite appearances to the contrary, or we reject it, and thereby exclude ourselves from the knowledge of his love willingly given to us.

Sometimes we come to realise that we have brought personal misfortune upon ourselves. Health may break down, for example, as the result of an inappropriate way of living, a relationship may fall apart due to unfaithfulness, and ambition may fail because it was born of self-centredness. Such instances arise out of our sinfulness: the refusal to consent to our own poverty before God, and surrender the control of our own lives to him, in order to let his life flow within us. Moments such as these, though, may become the points of entry for God if we recognise the truth of our condition and have the courage to let go of our pride and offer our empty hands to God in penitence, entrusting ourselves entirely to God's mercy and forgiveness.

This movement in our relationship with God is one which Jesus illustrated in one of the most celebrated of his parables, popularly known as The Prodigal Son.[5] It begins with the younger of the two sons asking his father for the share of his property The father allows himself to be vulnerable to his son, acceding to his own poverty, and as the story unfolds we may surmise that his son's request arose out of the belief that his ultimate security and happiness was to be found in material wealth. His experience, however, is a painful journey in self-discovery and growth in self-awareness, for having squandered his property, he comes to the realisation that he has nothing, indeed is nothing, and that he would be better off as one of his father's servants. The recognition of his complete poverty, expressed in the words 'I am no longer worthy to be called your son', enables him to entrust himself to his Father in complete penitence. He is met not with recrimination or anger, but with his father's desire to lavish his love upon him, and give all that he is and all that he has to him. The younger son's recognition and acceptance of his own poverty enables him to see what was true all along: that everything would have come to him anyway. It was his grasping, the refusal of his own poverty, which deprived him of what he wanted most of all.

The reaction of the elder brother in the story speaks to the condition of all those who believe themselves to be the seemingly innocent victims of the folly of others. The attitude towards his younger brother's adventures, and more particularly to the way in which he is treated on his return by his father, seems to be perfectly understandable and natural. Why after all should his brother be treated to such generosity when he himself has always behaved impeccably? The answer lies in his failure to appreciate that the father's desire to give is motivated not by the wish to reward good behaviour and punish the bad, but by sheer grace: the wanting to share all that he is and all that he has out of love alone. His attitudes and his actions make no difference whatsoever to those of his father: 'Son, you are always with me, and all that is mine is yours'. Unlike his brother he refuses to accept the truth of his own poverty, and to consent to it, and his self-right-eousness prevents him from realising the truth of his father's words.

In this parable Jesus gives us a story which is exquisite in the characterisation in the father of God's attitude towards us. The words spoken to the elder son are the words that God speaks to the whole of creation from the beginning: 'You are always with me, and all that is mine is yours'. It is for this reason that whether the recognition of our own poverty comes through our own folly, and in that sense seems acceptable, or through the ineptitude of others, and therefore seems unfair, is actually neither here nor there, for the gift of knowing that in our poverty God is everything to us far outweighs the manner in which we are brought to that realisation. Whatever our circum-stances, whatever happens to us, the truth is that at every moment, in every circumstance God is seeking to entrust himself to us if we will allow him to. St Paul expressed the awareness of this truth as follows:

'I am convinced that neither death, nor life, nor angels, nor rulers, nor things present, nor things to come, nor powers, nor height, nor depth, nor anything else in all creation, will be able to separate us from the love of God in Christ Jesus our Lord.'[6]

The dawning of that awareness came to St Paul only as with pain and trauma he came to recognise and consent to his own poverty. Looked at from his perspective what happened could scarcely have been anticipated, but from the perspective of poverty, human and divine, it was almost inevitable. The recognition of poverty came to St. Paul when he saw that the very things upon which he prided himself as gifts from God himself, and signs of his favour, were the same things which excluded God. He came to see that he placed his trust not in God, but in himself, and was consequently living an illusion.

Clearly he was a highly respected member of Jewish society, born with immense social privileges, highly educated, and extremely influential. Furthermore, he applauded his own sense of moral achievement, which was precisely what blinded him to the truth of his own condition, for he came to perceive that he was to be instrumental in saving his Jewish faith from corruption at the hands of the followers of Jesus. Thus he persecuted those first Christians and conspired to bring about their deaths. The morally upright, sophisticated, devout Pharisee became consumed with a hatred, a hardness of heart, and an unswerving and passionate belief in the rightness of his cause. The reduction to poverty led him to see how far he was from the truth.

The experience of conversion, through the encounter with the Risen Christ on the Damascus Road,[7] undergirds everything that Paul wrote as the central, most significant and formative experience of his life. With hindsight he could appreciate it as such, but at the time it must have been bewildering, disorientating and humiliating. The experience revealed to him that in relation to God what he considered to be his riches counted for nothing, indeed that they could inculcate in him a false sense of security. At the moment of his encounter with the Risen Lord they were of no use to him whatsoever.

The experience of poverty for Paul was total. His learning as a Pharisee could not enable him initially to identify who it was that was meeting him. In response to the question 'Saul, Saul, why are you persecuting me?' all Saul could reply was 'Who are you Lord?' The knowledge upon which Saul had prided himself was of no consequence when brought into living contact with the truth, indeed it blinded him to the truth.

It is for that reason not entirely coincidental that Paul's spiritual blindness was made known to him through physical blindness. Deprived of sight he was utterly dependent upon others, and the great crusader had to be taken by the hand like a child and brought to Damascus. There the great activist in the service of the Lord was forced to wait in darkness, powerless to do anything at all, even perhaps to understand what had really happened to him.

It was God himself for whom Paul had to wait, and in order to receive God Paul had to consent to his coming at the hands of Ananias, one whom Paul's natural inclination would have been to despise. In relation to Ananias Paul had to learn of and accept his poverty, for there is no indication that Ananias was especially learned. Paul had to acknowledge that in such matters the most simple person of all may know far more about the things of God than one endowed with great learning. As he received the laying on of hands from Ananias so he received the life of God into himself:

'So Ananias went and entered the house. He laid his hands on Saul and said, "Brother Saul, the Lord Jesus, who appeared to you on your way here, has sent me so that you may regain your sight and be filled with the Holy Spirit." And immediately something like scales fell from his eyes, and his sight was restored. Then he got up and was baptized, and after taking some food, he regained his strength.'[8]

It is tempting to assume that the outcome of Paul's experience was a foregone conclusion, and that in some way his own freedom was overridden, but that would be to misinterpret. Our own experience can help us to understand what it must have been like for Paul, for the immediate reaction which we all share in the face of our own weakness and poverty is to resist and fight it: we refuse to consent to what is happening to us. It is only when we accept it in its totality that we are able to receive from God what he is seeking to give us in and through it. Paul could well have resisted his impoverishment. He could have refused to look in to what had stopped him in his tracks and what lay behind his blindness and tried to carry on in spite of what had happened. It is impossible to conjecture what might have become of him had that been the case, but it is not inconceivable that he would have remained embittered, resentful, angry, and in a real sense, dead. He had to consent to the truth of his poverty if he was to be refashioned.

Such consent must have come to him in the realisation that in refusing to acknowledge his poverty he was not only separating himself from God, but also, precisely because of that, alienating himself from his own true self, which was grounded in God, by shutting off the flow of God's life in him. It is highly significant, therefore, that the consent that Paul made resulted in receiving new life in the Spirit. It was this that enabled him to enter into the awareness of his own true nature, which he expressed as follows:

'I have been crucified with Christ; and it is no longer I who live, but it is Christ who lives in me.'[9]

With hindsight Paul was able to speak of his experience as being the most creative of his life:

'Whatever gains I had, these I have come to regard as loss because of Christ. More than that, I regard everything as loss because of the surpassing value of knowing Christ Jesus my Lord. For his sake I have suffered the loss of all things, and I regard them as rubbish, in order that I may gain Christ and be found in him.'[10]

St. Paul's experience is one in which we can perceive the central thrust of God's creative purposes: that God brings all things into being in the Word, who is made flesh in Christ, and enlivens us in that Word, in Christ, by the Holy Spirit. The truth is staggering in its simplicity, and yet we find it so hard not only to understand it, but to receive it and live it, indeed Paul's experience reveals that ultimately it may even be our understanding, our supposed knowledge that acts as a barrier between us and God. Crises of faith, therefore, when we are no longer able to pray, when God seems to disappear, when we can no longer make sense of things as we used to, are not to be approached as we so often think, by clinging to the familiar, believing that thereby we shall be secure. Rather the path ahead lies in the often painful acceptance of our poverty, our inability to do or be anything at all on our own, for hidden in the darkness, as in the darkness of the womb, the Holy Spirit is secretly, mysteriously at work, impregnating us with the life of Christ, and transforming us into him. This is what God is seeking to do all the time. By concealing himself he places within us the awareness of mystery, which is revealed in time as the mystery of Christ. In his love God entrusts the realisation of that mystery in us to our willingness to consent to our poverty. In the moment that we consent, and entrust ourselves to God, we enter into the awareness that in our nothingness God is our fullness, in our poverty we are rich beyond measure.

CHAPTER FOUR

Inspiring

Then afterwards baptized I was:
The Holy Ghost on me did glance,
My Father's voice heard from above,
To call my true love to my dance:
Sing O my love, O my love, my love, my love;
This have I done for my true love.

The moment of birth, like the moment of death, is profoundly mysterious, for it is then, perhaps more than at any other time, that we are aware that we have no ultimate control over our existence. With Job we can say:

'Naked I came from my mother's womb, and naked shall I return there; the Lord gave and the Lord has taken away; blessed be the name of the Lord.'[1]

For some people, of course, the two moments, the two extremities of birth and death, come together. It is not as frequent now as in years gone past but it still occasionally happens that a mother dies while giving birth to her child. Sadly it is rather more frequent than that that the child itself may be stillborn, or dies soon after birth. Such an event is deeply sad, although never beyond redemption. It is still possible in such circumstances for God to give himself if allowed to do so. The stillbirth of her firstborn child was for one mother the very means by which she became aware of what was important in life, and what was not, and within a year she decided to be confirmed, thus acknowledging for herself the life of God within her that had been acknowledged by others on her behalf at her baptism many years before as a child.

In spite of the redemptive possibilities in all circum-

46

stances nobody could ever wish the grief caused by the loss of life at birth on another. Worse than the grief is the loss itself, the emptiness left by what might have been. Fortunately, where my own children are concerned we have not suffered such loss. The births of our first two children were scarcely plain sailing: with the first my wife required an epidural and with the second concern was expressed at the length of the labour to the extent that preparations were made for delivery by Caesarean section, which in the event was unnecessary. The births of our third and fourth children were much less difficult, the last being the easiest of all. So straightforward was it that it was only two minutes or so after the moment of birth that it occurred to us to ask whether it was a boy or a girl, and much to our surprise we learned that after three boys the fourth was in fact a girl. It would not have made any difference to us either way: our attitude was like that of so many other parents in simply wanting a healthy baby. Our only significant trauma in relation to the health of our children came six months later when our daughter became seriously ill and, but for an emergency operation, would have died.

It was the actual birth of our third child that brought me closest to the related mystery of birth and death. All four of our children were very much wanted, but the third assumed a unique significance in that we believed that after our second child it would not be possible to have any more children. My wife had contracted Pelvic Inflammatory Disease, the consequence of which was that conception was no longer possible, and for which the cure was to have a baby! As if by a miracle a child was conceived and his birth was anticipated with great excitement.

At the moment of delivery it seemed as though our hopes were to be dashed. Towards the end of the labour we sensed that something was wrong because the umbilical cord was being cut before he had been fully delivered. The cord in fact had become entwined around his neck. As he emerged he was blue and lifeless. My immediate reaction was that he was dead. Momentarily I experienced a profound sense of loss, above all that we would never know the child. It would seem as if he had never been and it would be difficult to give him an identity. For a minute or so nothing happened, and then eventually there was the sound of an involuntary inhalation of breath, followed by the first sounds of crying, and he became a living being, with whom there was already a relationship, and whom we were able to call by the name we had chosen for him. His life, his identity, depended entirely upon that first inhalation of breath, upon in-spir-ation.

Who we are depends upon inspiration, the breathing into us of the Holy Spirit of life, who enlivens us at every level of our being, body, mind and spirit. It was at his baptism when Jesus received the Holy Spirit more deeply and more fully, that he came to the realisation, humanly speaking, of his true identity as the Eternal Son of God, an identity that had been waiting to be realised from the moment of conception, as the words of the angel to Mary indicate:

'The Holy Spirit will come upon you, and the power of the Most High will overshadow you; therefore the child to be born will be holy; he will be called Son of God'.[2]

It is, of course, impossible to know exactly what occurred to Jesus as he was baptized, but whatever the case it was clearly a watershed. The accounts in the Synoptic Gospels simply point towards its deeper, hidden truth and meaning:

'In those days Jesus came from Nazareth of Galilee and was baptized by John in the Jordan. And just as he was coming up out of the water, he saw the heavens torn apart and the Spirit descending like a dove on him. And a voice came from heaven, "You are my Son, the Beloved; with you I am well pleased".'[3]

With the baptismal experience Jesus not only entered into the realisation of his own identity; he disclosed the ultimate nature of God, and indeed of our identity in him, too. This nature is none other than love itself ("You are my Son, the Beloved"). Jesus knew himself as forever returning to the Father in the Spirit of love. It was the Holy Spirit, flooding Jesus with love, which gave him the awareness and realisation of his unique identity, value and worth, enabling him to know himself as the object, the recipient of infinite and eternal love, deeply personal in character. In this love he knew himself to be Son, and the source of love as Father. Not only did he know himself as forever coming from the Father in the Spirit of love, he knew himself as forever returning to the Father in the Spirit of love, too. In the depths of his being he knew himself to be grounded in a relationship, in which there is distinction and yet total unity. In this relationship there is a rhythm, a dance, consisting of an eternal giving and receiving of love in complete union: communion. It is this relationship which lies at the heart of all things, and in which all things are grounded, and which the whole of creation is to realise: all things participate in this coming from the Father, through the Son, in the Spirit, and in the Spirit return to the Father through the Son.

The language of Trinitarian doctrine is highly inadequate, as is all language about God. It seeks to express rationally in concepts that which lies infinitely beyond them. The doctrine of the Trinity symbolises for us the experience of the reality that transcends all words and formulae. The way in which we enter into the experience which it symbolises is to do none other than share in Jesus' own awareness and experience. This is not something that anyone else can do for us, nor does it consist in only knowing about it or understanding it. It is a profoundly intuitive experience in which we grow, until with St Paul, following Jesus himself, we can say:

'God has sent the Spirit of his Son into our hearts, crying, "Abba! Father!"'[4]

It is not simply that we seek to enter into the experience

of Jesus' baptism alone. We enter into the totality of his
life experience, his way of being, living and loving, and
thereby enter into that intuitive awareness of our relationship with the Father through the Son in the Spirit. The
whole purpose of the creative process is for us to realise
this truth. Everything, therefore, our total life experience,
is capable of leading us to it.

We know precious little of how Jesus himself was
brought to the realisation of his own identity. Precisely
because of that it may not be unreasonable to assume that
up to his baptism his experience was unexceptional, otherwise it would most certainly have been of interest and
commented upon. The only suggestion we have is in St.
Luke's Gospel concerning the incident in the temple at
twelve years of age.[5] What seems to lie behind this is
evidence of a young boy of considerable spiritual sensitivity, searching for answers to questions among the
teachers of his religious tradition. It may well be that he
was seeking to compare his own already heightened and
advanced awareness with that of the tradition, for it is
suggested that what he communicated to them prompted
amazement at his understanding and answers. To which,
of course, we must note the observation, that to have gone
astray, so it seemed to others, for three days, and not to be
concerned, is in itself remarkable. Other than this episode,
though, we know nothing of Jesus' development into
adulthood, to the point where at his baptism he came to
know who he truly was.

How, then, did Jesus come to the knowledge of his own
identity? We may presume that four factors were involved,
none of them unique to Jesus, all of which are necessary
for anyone to realise their own identity. These are: relationships, the development of personal gifts and abilities,
the participation in a spiritual tradition, and the direct but
hidden action of the Holy Spirit.

First, relationships. There can be little doubt that Jesus'
family was important for him in coming to the knowledge

of his identity, as it is for anyone else. What happens from the moment of birth onwards influences what kind of people we become. If we are fortunate we grow up knowing that we are loved, that we are of value and importance, that we matter to others, that our very existence makes a difference. So, too, we learn to love others in return. In relation to others we learn or fail to learn what is acceptable behaviour, what it is that increases the sense of worth that we have of ourselves and of others, and what diminishes it. We come to know our capacity for selfishness or selflessness, we discover moral values and the significance of community, the place of forgiveness and compassion, and of the longing for union.

There is little of any particularity that we can say of Jesus' experience in this area, except that behind all that is communicated to us in the gospels is the awareness of the fact of Jesus' family, and especially the place of his mother. It would not be unreasonable to assume that one who was so open, warm, selfless and loving in his own relationships at least learnt some of this within his family, even though it is quite clear that he saw beyond the limitation of family ties, and indeed perceived that they could be a barrier to the realisation of our ultimate identity.

Secondly, it is the growth and development of personal gifts and abilities which give us a sense of our own identity. The nurturing of these things comes largely through education, with the support of family and friends. We develop physically, emotionally, intellectually and socially, and characteristics are manifested in us in a unique way. We discover our natural abilities, along with our strengths and weaknesses. Skills learnt through schooling enable us to explore the world, to delight in it and contribute to it. The capacity to express ourselves is encouraged through the artistic imagination as well as through the ability to think, reflect, discriminate and evaluate. Science enables us to investigate the nature of the physical universe, and to use our knowledge to practical advantage. Through this process of education we begin to discover just what our gifts and abilities are, and how we can use them in such a way that contributes to the sense of who we are. This is a major factor in the educational process, the awakening to what we are to be and to do in and with our lives, and all that they entail, in order to take our place in society.

Again we know next to nothing for sure about this aspect of Jesus' development. We may presume that like any other child of his background and culture he will have learnt the family trade. Beyond that his adult identity reveals a highly developed imaginative faculty, as his parables prove, as well as an incisive intellect, as some of his encounters with his opponents show.[6] Further than this we are aware that he was extraordinarily gifted as a teacher and communicator, as a leader and motivator, as a listener, healer and more. All this contributed to his sense of identity.

Thirdly, the spiritual tradition in which we grow has a significant influence on our formation. Jesus was born a Jew and was clearly well acquainted with the whole tradition in which he stood. He was in the habit of attending the synagogue and the temple, he knew the scriptures, and was able to interpret them with more subtlety than many of the official representatives of the tradition. He had the awareness of God which the Jewish tradition sought to mediate, but he was also critical of it, having an intuitive sense of what lay at the heart of it. In spite of this he had no official place in the institutional life of his religion, and was ultimately condemned by it; yet he was completely assured in his handling of it.

Our conscious knowledge of God comes largely by participation in a spiritual tradition. For most people, whatever their faith, religion is bound up with cultural and national identity, too. The spiritual tradition has a significant influence on the values and beliefs of a society. Our spiritual consciousness is formed in the context of the tradition itself. We allow ourselves to be drawn into the experience of all those who have been part of, and who have helped to shape, the tradition. Their experience points us in the direction of God, invites us to stand where they stood in order to know God as they did. This is true of any spiritual tradition. For Christians, however, the one in whose shoes they stand, as it were, the one through whom their spiritual consciousness is formed, is Jesus himself. Through prayer and the sacraments, through study and meditation on the scriptures, through reflection on the tradition in its past and present forms, and by participating in the community life which affirms the tradition, we are drawn more deeply into the experience of Jesus himself, and share in his spiritual consciousness.

The last factor that influences the realisation of our identity is the direct action of the Holy Spirit himself. There can be little doubt that where Jesus himself was concerned this was more significant than any of the others. His family may have been instrumental in his development, but the knowledge of his identity was not dependent upon that relationship. Where his own gifts and abilities are concerned there is no doubt that he was highly developed, but he is not known and remembered, nor was the consciousness of his own identity, primarily as a teacher, an orator, a healer or anything else. Certainly he embraced them, but in his deepest identity he far transcended them. Even where his spiritual tradition was concerned it is clear that he was formed within it, but it could hardly be said that his identity was confined to or by it. Rather it was through him that the possibility of reshaping and transforming it was offered. Instead he was rejected by it.

When we seek to enter into Jesus' spiritual consciousness we can follow the three preceding routes up to a point but they only take us so far, for the simple reason that the ground of his consciousness, his deepest identity, transcends them all. Indeed when we really think about it is hard to believe that in the absence of the direct influence of the Holy Spirit he could have been what he was at all. So whole a person does he seem to have been that something else has to be accounted for. It is the Holy Spirit which does so account. Beyond all those things which shape and form our identities Jesus knew himself primarily in his relationship with God. It was the Holy Spirit in the depths of his being who confirmed his identity as Son, and in the Holy Spirit he knew himself to be grounded in a relationship of personal love with one known to him as Father. This is the significance of the baptism. He had been formed in the context of a family, his own gifts and abilities had been allowed to come to light, he had imbibed his spiritual tradition, but it was only in going beyond them that he realised his deepest identity. It is no coincidence that baptism should have brought this about, and that it was after having gone under the water that he knew who he was in the Spirit, for the ritual immersion signified a leaving behind of everything that had formed his identity up to that point. Jesus' baptism was indeed for him a death, in which he renounced the self which was limited in its identity, and went beyond such limitation, to awaken, to be born in the Spirit to his real identity as Son of the Father.

Paradoxically it is the conferring of our own identity by the direct inspiration of the Holy Spirit which, certainly in the western world, is likely to elude us more than anything else. If we ask ourselves who we are, and what is the nature of our identity, our instinctive reaction is very likely to define ourselves by what we do, by our role in society or by our family relationships. We may define ourselves by our political or religious allegiance, or by the identification with some cause or other, or by cultural or national identity, but these are all temporary, transient and limited. If we define ourselves in such ways it is all the more so that in the western world fewer people affirm the importance of a spiritual tradition in the formation and realisation of identity, and fewer still the direct inspiration of the Holy Spirit. Yet the fact is for all of us that none of the other influences is capable of guaranteeing and bringing us to our ultimate identity, for they all pass away. It is only in relation to God that we know ourselves as existing in eternity.

How, then, do we come to know this identity? By going beyond all limitation, by transcending our identification with anything in the world, to find ourselves in God, to know ourselves as words in the Eternal Word, as coming from the Father through the Son in the Spirit, and returning to the Father in the Spirit through the Son. The whole creative process brings us to the point where we have to go through all created forms, beyond thought and concepts to a direct, intuitive experience of God. Jesus is supremely the one in whom and through whom we are taken beyond all things to the Father, for he is the Way, the Truth and the Life.[7] The way to life and truth is through none other than death:

'If any want to become my followers, let them deny themselves and take up their cross daily and follow me. For those who want to save their life will lose it, and those who lose their life for my sake will save it. What does it profit them if they gain the whole world, but lose or forfeit themselves?'[8]

This is the significance of our own baptism. We die to everything in this world, to all limitation and restriction, and depend entirely upon the Holy Spirit to bring us to life in Christ. The way to this truth is by baptism into his death, so that we may live with his life.

It is possible for us to become aware of this identity at any time and in any place, but usually we are given an intimation of it in and through some experience of loss, whether of relationship, job, reputation, health or whatever. If our sense of identity has rested upon such a thing its loss may bring us to the awareness that we are more than that. If we cling to what has been taken away we only enhance the frustration at the loss of identity, and we search for it where it cannot be found. If we freely let go, though, we discover that an identity grounded in something beyond emerges. Ultimately we discover this identity to be grounded in God.

The awareness of our true identity in such circumstances emerges as we are deprived of our partial identity. We need not wait for such occurrences, however. We can indeed go beyond all limited identities quite freely and consciously as a matter of choice. The path we follow is that of meditation. Here is a way which enables us to pass quite deliberately beyond thought, concept, idea and form, to an intuitive awareness of our grounding in God. There are many ways to meditate, the most common involving the saying of a mantra. By this means the mind is brought to rest and stillness and we become conscious that we are more than anything that we can think. Beyond that we become aware that we are grounded in God.

In all spiritual traditions simply observing the breath leads us beyond our limited consciousness, and within the Christian tradition this is especially appropriate because of the association of breath with wind and spirit. Observation of the breath does not involve thinking about it, still less trying to breathe. All that is necessary is an attentive awareness, in which we observe the inhalation of breath, which is the means by which we receive life, and the exhalation of breath, which is the means by which we yield up our life in death. If we simply allow ourselves to breathe our awareness expands until eventually, identified with no created thing, we become aware that it is not we breathing at all, it is another, from whom we come, and to whom we return. We become aware that in the ground of our being we participate in a relationship of love, in which all things are held. We know that our identity is in God, who is beyond all things, yet present in all things. We discover ourselves to exist in God, coming from the Father, through the Son, in the Spirit, and returning to the Father, in the Spirit, through the Son. With St. Paul we enter into the experience of Jesus himself and in the Spirit we know ourselves in the Son, and our whole being breathes 'Abba, Father'. It is an identity which is beyond created form, and is grounded in God. Indeed we know that we are an idea in the mind of God, a word existing in the Word, which is enfleshed, incarnated in the particular person that we are.

This is the awareness that lies behind Jeremiah's experience:

'Now the word of the Lord came to me saying, "Before I formed you in the womb I knew you, and before you were born I consecrated you".'[9]

St Paul, too, seems to have been led to a similar awareness, which he expresses in the Letter to the Galatians:

'God ... set me apart before I was born and called me through his grace.'[10]

Nor is this awareness unique, unusual or esoteric; the ultimate identity of all is to be discovered in it, as the opening of the Letter to the Ephesians suggests:

'Blessed be the God and Father of our Lord Jesus Christ, who has blessed us in Christ with every spiritual blessing in the heavenly places, just as he chose us in Christ before the foundation of the world to be holy and blameless before him in love. He destined us for adoption as his children through Jesus Christ, according to the good pleasure of his will, to the praise of his glorious grace that he freely bestowed on us in the Beloved. In him we have redemption through his blood, the forgiveness of our trespasses, according to the riches of his grace that he lavished on us. With all wisdom and insight he has made known to us the mystery of his will, according to his good pleasure that he set forth in Christ, as a plan for the fullness of time, to gather up all things in him, things in heaven and things on earth. In Christ we have also obtained an inheritance, having been destined according to the purpose of him who accomplishes all things according to his counsel and will, so that we, who were the first to set our hope on Christ, might live for the praise of his glory.'[11]

When we attain to this realisation everything is transformed. The world which we have left behind is now seen in its true identity in the Son, expressive of the Word. The whole of creation breathes 'Abba' in the Spirit through Christ. No longer do we see anything or anyone in its partial identity, but in its ultimate identity in God. Everything and everyone is known to participate in an eternal dance of love at the heart of all things, and we know that we exist for that sole reason. We know, too, that birth and death are separated only by the tiniest space in the breath, and in that space the Holy Spirit is present, waiting to inspire us with the realisation of our ultimate identity in Christ.

CHAPTER FIVE

Withdrawing

Into the desert I was led,
Where I fasted without substance;
The devil bade me make stones my bread,
To have me break my true love's dance:
Sing O my love, O my love, my love, my love:
This have I done for my true love.

I sit at a desk and write in a room which measures twelve feet by nine feet. The room also contains a bed, a bedside table, a prayer desk, an armchair, a washbasin and a cupboard. The basic requirements of life are reduced to a minimum. It is a much simpler and less cluttered lifestyle than I am accustomed to, but, for a period of two months this is my home, where, for the most part, I write and pray. It is housed in a convent, the home of a contemplative community of sisters, and it is my privilege to join them in the daily round of the singing of the monastic offices and the celebration of the Eucharist. I eat lunch and high tea with them in the refectory, and my only contribution to the practical requirements of community life is to assist with washing up after meals.

My day has a certain basic rhythm. I rise quite early, at about 6.15 a.m. (although not quite as early as the sisters who rise in time to sing Lauds at 6.10 a.m.), and after washing and dressing I meditate for an hour or so. After I have breakfasted I write for a while, or allow myself some time and space for what is to be given expression in the written word to emerge. The Office of Terce begins at 9.00 a.m., and is followed by the Eucharist, and for the two hours which are then available before Sext at Midday, and lunch, I continue to write, either beginning or ending with a walk in the locality lasting half an hour. I may rest briefly after lunch, but sometimes I use the ensuing period of nearly four-and-a-half hours (punctuated with None at 2.00 p.m.) as an opportunity for extended writing. Depending on the stage I have reached I may meditate for an hour before Vespers, which takes place at 5.30 p.m., or if I am in full flow I continue to write up until Vespers and meditate later on in the evening instead. In between High Tea, which is eaten straight after Vespers at about 6.00 p.m., and Compline, the final office of the day, at 8.00 p.m., I either write, or I may read a novel for a while or listen to some music or to a programme on the radio, and the same applies to the remaining two hours or so after Compline has ended; and then I retire to bed soon after 10.00 p.m.

The life of the community is directed solely to the worship of and attention to God. Its members have in one sense withdrawn from the everyday world in order to live this life of singular devotion, but it would be quite wrong to assume that this implies a rejection of the world. Rather the total commitment to God leads to the rediscovery of the world in its true life and depth, indeed as the expression of the life and love of God, and the world and its concerns are seen and known in their joy and delight, as well as in their pain and anguish. This awareness is acknowledged in the time given to the costly and selfless prayer of intercession, which occupies a significant amount of the sisters' attention. So, too, does the hospitality extended to the steady stream of guests reveal an attitude that embraces the world, not only rejoicing with those whose path leads them to the fullness of life, but also taking into itself the tensions and sorrows of those in need. It is to share in this life of withdrawal that I have come.

The key to the awareness of God, and to the rediscovery of the world in depth, is silence. Silence pervades the life of the community in all its facets. It is out of silence that words and actions emerge, that God is known, that love is born, from which healing comes, and in which attention is given to the world. External silence reflects and leads to inner silence in turn, so that silence becomes a habit of the body, mind and spirit, in which all things are held together. In this inner solitude we become deeply aware of the fact that our overwhelming desire is for God, but our withdrawal from the world reveals all too clearly, also, that we are very much part of the world, that we bring it in with us in what and who we are, with all our faults, tensions, anxieties and blockages, as well as with what we might become when we allow the Spirit fully to bring us to life in Christ. It is then that we realise that withdrawal is not an escape: it is an encounter with truth, the truth of God, of the world, and of ourselves. In essence, then, to withdraw is to allow God the opportunity to realise his life in us more fully. It can only be on the understanding, however, that this necessarily involves us in becoming aware of the ways in which we inhibit that life. Rarely is this easy or painless, and there are times when the knowledge and awareness of the love of God is coupled with a painful self-knowledge which is almost too much to bear, and from which we are tempted to do almost anything to escape.

The main purpose for my being here is to write, for which I have been given an opportunity to withdraw from my day to day concerns and responsibilities. It is paradoxical, but true nevertheless, that it is only through withdrawal, through separation and detachment, that we discover that all things are one, and that what unites them is prayer. Prayer is not primarily something which we do, or make happen, or initiate. It is happening all the time within us, for it is none other than the life of God, and God invites us freely to let it happen, to let him breathe his Spirit of life and love in us through his Son, to be returned in love to him. Prayer is the dance of love which is the life of God the Holy Trinity. Within the Holy Trinity prayer is the love shared between the Father and the Son in the Spirit. We participate in this prayer as we allow ourselves to be drawn into this mutual exchange of love, and it is the Spirit who prays within us. St Paul knew this only too well:

'Likewise the Spirit helps us in our weakness; for we do not know how to pray as we ought, but that very Spirit intercedes with sighs too deep for words. And God, who searches the heart, knows what is the mind of the Spirit, because the Spirit intercedes for the saints according to the will of God.'[1]

In the life of the community there are set times of prayer, both corporate and solitary, but it is not the case that these are the only times when prayer is happening. Rather they are the times when we consciously align ourselves with that rhythm of life and love in which we participate in the Spirit, in order to realise, to be aware, to see more clearly that everything lives and breathes in the prayer of the Trinity. This is a truth into which the very activity of writing leads me more deeply, but not without discomfort.

It is ironic that I have looked forward to this opportunity to write for some time, and yet, now that I have it, there are times when I should prefer to be doing almost anything else at all. Not only are there moments of dissatisfaction; there are also periods of near paralysis when nothing seems to come, or, if it does, it is in fits and starts, requiring an effort out of all proportion to the results. At such moments I am besieged by doubts as to whether it is the right thing to be doing at all and I question my motives. The descent continues into greater darkness when I am tormented by the prospect that this precious time is simply being wasted, and that I should have done something much more worthwhile. I persuade myself that I shall have achieved nothing at all except complete an exercise in self-delusion. The deeper I descend, the worse the matter becomes, and as I try harder and harder so less and less is expressed.

In the darkest moments, when it is tempting to give up altogether, I am reminded, and I have to learn again, that the solution lies not in running away but in letting go. Running away means that the real problem remains unresolved: it is simply left to emerge in another way sometime in the future. Furthermore running away is only an attempt to hide from the sense of inner emptiness and poverty into some form of distraction, which promises to bring relief, but which is only ever temporary. It can be humiliating to discover the trifling things with which we are prepared to trade off our discomfort: something to eat or drink, a programme on the radio, a book or a newspaper. It is not that such things are bad; the significance lies in the purpose to which we put them, and when we have withdrawn from our everyday concerns it becomes all too clear how much we use many things simply as a distraction from the emptiness within us.

Letting go, on the other hand, requires a complete acceptance of my total inability to produce anything at all. It involves an inner surrender, an acknowledgement that all I can do is wait, and allow time and space for something to emerge from deep within. I abandon my self-imposed timetable and give up trying to force anything at all. I meditate, in which I seek to let go of self-centredness, of the sense of my separation from God and from my deepest self. Often I come out of a period of meditation feeling integrated, with a renewed perspective, which leads me to the realisation that the cause of my creative sterility has arisen from being focused too much on my self and not enough on God.

So it is that I perceive that my writing is related to God, in fact it is prayer, or it is nothing at all. In this sense it is no different from anything else, it is only the form of activity and expression that differentiates, for in writing, as in anything else, the sole intention is to be fully attentive to God in the present moment. God seeks to give expression to his creative Word in creation and in me. He can only do so if I allow him to, which requires that my essential attitude in writing is to be one of an attentive passivity, a surrender in the Spirit, which is prayer. By means of writing I desire the Father to enflesh his Word in my words, and since my overwhelming desire is that this should be so, the offering of myself is at the same time a returning to him of his Word in a spirit of adoration. My wish is that God should be glorified in and through me.

So my writing becomes far more than simply trying to cover pages with words, or an attempt to achieve or gain adulation. It is prayer, in which I seek to be open to the Spirit, to let him make the Word flesh in me as an act of love and praise for the Creator. The secondary desire is that those who read what I write will thereby be drawn in some small way into that same life of prayer which lies at the heart of God. In this way I am aware that all activity, all life, is potentially prayer.

Other factors have a bearing on my awareness of writing as prayer, not least my body. My body is a very powerful indicator of my overall state of being. There are the obvious tensions caused by the posture necessitated by writing; the shoulders and the neck become stiff, for example. Such tensions reveal something far more subtle, however, for the body communicates and reflects the degree of openness or closedness to the Spirit which prevails within me. A headache generally suggests that I am trying too hard, indeed that what I am writing is coming only from the head rather than from the inner depths. Sometimes I discover that my shoulders are hunched, but by far the most revealing is that my stomach and diaphragm are tense, indicating that I am holding on and in, interrupting the natural rhythm of the breath, and thus inhibiting the Spirit. Paying attention to my body is, like writing, prayer, because I seek to discover where I am inhibiting the flow of life in me, which my body registers. It is also in accordance with St Paul's injunction, to make my body available to God for his creative purposes, as well as my mind and spirit:

'I appeal to you therefore, brothers and sisters, by the

mercies of God, to present your bodies as a living sacrifice, holy and acceptable to God, which is your spiritual worship. Do not be conformed to this world, but be transformed by the renewing of your minds, so that you may discern what is the will of God – what is good and acceptable and perfect.'[2]

My body always plays an integral role in meditation. It is not that the relaxation of the body is a mere aid to meditation, rather it is the case that by integrating the body with the mind and spirit the whole person is given to the action of the Spirit:

'Do you not know that your body is a temple of the Holy Spirit within you, which you have from God, and that you are not your own? For you were bought with a price; therefore glorify God in your body.'[3]

In western culture there is a tendency to regard the body as something that we possess rather than as part of what we are. The essential harmony of body, mind and spirit is ignored, even where physical exercise and activity is valued. The body tends to be treated as a machine which is to be controlled and disciplined. Behind this appears to lie a mistrust and fear of the body, a suspicion that if left to its own devices we shall be overcome by powerful and uncontrollable forces, not least the sexual energy. Such an attitude, however, seems to stem from a view that separates the body from the rest of our being, rather than accepts that body, mind and spirit are a unity. Then the body is not abandoned to its own devices, for ultimately it has no devices which are separate from the rest of our being. Indeed it is only when the spiritual nature of the body is ignored that it is uncontrollable. In meditation, however, the body is treated far more gently, attention being paid to its delicate balance, so that even the smallest thing can communicate something significant. Above all the attitude to the body in meditation is that it should be relaxed in an alert and conscious way. The overall attitude of the mind influences the extent to which the body is relaxed or not, and relaxation is primarily letting go of tension in order to let the natural flow of life be free. That flow of life comes in the Holy Spirit, so to be free in the body is to be drawn into freedom at every level of our being, in a receptivity towards the Holy Spirit.

Meditation and writing are in one sense separate activities, but they are part of a greater unity together which is prayer, and in that prayer each has an influence on the other. It is not only during the times of meditation that I seek to be attentive to God, and to my body. I seek to live in the awareness of God, and to be relaxed in body when I am writing, and at all other times, too. Every aspect of life is then seen in the context of life's ultimate purpose, which is by every means to be drawn into the life and love of the Trinity, and to be expressive of that life.

Paradoxically, then, the time of withdrawal enhances within me the awareness of the essential unity of all things in God. For that reason other things impinge upon my awareness which relate to my everyday concerns and responsibilities, and it is the very awareness of God made possible in withdrawal which makes me more acutely aware of the ways in which I interrupt the flow of the Spirit in the rest of my life. As I pray for the people in my parish I become aware of mistakes and failures in my attitudes and relationships, of the extent to which I have acted as a barrier to the Holy Spirit. Past hurts and embarrassments come to light once again, and I am reminded of my own weaknesses. My eyes are also opened, though, to the immense goodness and love of so many, and I wonder how I can be more available to God so that I will not be a barrier to his work of bringing them into the fullness of life. I question much of what I have done and wonder about my future ministry.

Most of all, perhaps, I am aware of my family. I spend the weekends with them but I realise that my absence during the week puts a pressure on them, especially on my wife. I am besieged with feelings of guilt at times, and I wonder whether my period of withdrawal might not after all be an indulgence of self-interest. At times I question whether I should not simply return home, but I know that my wife would selflessly not agree to that.

The weekends with the family, though, are part of the rhythm of withdrawal. Being away from them in the week heightens my awareness of them when we are together. The enhanced sensitivity to the unity of all things in God, which withdrawal produces, opens me to the presence of God in them, a presence which is known in relationship. Almost as if for the first time I become conscious that God is seeking to dance his love in them, and that I can contribute to their being open or closed to him. The time of withdrawal makes me deeply conscious of how preoccupation with other things in the past has disabled me from being attentive to God's presence in them. I marvel that my little daughter shrieks with delight when she sees me again, that she jumps up into my arms and squeezes me, her eyes dancing with life, her face transparent with joy. I wonder at the sheer resilience which has not been beaten down into apathy by my failures to be attentive to her, and my newly-found awareness of her rebounds on me as I realise that I obviously matter to her as much as she matters to me. My attentiveness enables me to see the life and the love that flows between us, and, in seeing, I am encouraged to respond even more, and so the Spirit is allowed greater scope.

My youngest son, too, invites me into his world with such frequency that I ask myself how often he feels that I have excluded him in the past simply by failing to notice. More than anything else he just wants me to be with him, to do some colouring, or to look at a book, to go to the swings or to play with a ball. Play becomes holy by allowing the Spirit to be the bond of love flowing between us, and in the Spirit we both become more fully alive.

My other sons are older and their needs are different, but what is required is my inner availability to them, my affirmation of them to be themselves, the withdrawal of my hopes for and expectations of them, the encouragement of them to discover their own unique identity, how it is that God is seeking to live his life in them. The underlying withdrawal here lies in the willingness to decrease, to be there as and when they want me, to let them be free to grow in their own way, not resenting it when I appear to be redundant, nor withholding support when it is requested.

It is my wife who carries the burden of my withdrawal from the family week by week, and the deeper awareness that I have of God, of myself and of others, most of all embraces her. I notice how little space, internal or external, our lifestyle affords her, and with what generosity she accepts that. For that to be different will require changes in me, and I am fearful that when this period of extended withdrawal comes to a close it will be so easy to slip into old habits once again. I can see that she needs an opportunity to withdraw, too, if the Spirit is not to be stifled in her. If the presence of God is diminished in her, then it is also diminished in me, for it is the Spirit who is the bond of love between us. The withdrawal from parochial responsibilities which I enjoy at the moment has to find a way of remaining part of our lifestyle in the parish if my wife is to be given the opportunity to withdraw too.

The external withdrawal brings all this to light, but it serves as a reminder that withdrawal is really a way of being at any time and in any situation, for it is none other than the removal of all that occludes the presence of God and obstructs the free flow of the Spirit. To withdraw, then, is to withdraw into our own spirit where the Holy Spirit is present within us, so that he might dance within, between and among us.

Withdrawal was clearly a feature of Jesus' life, and something he encouraged in others. Luke, especially characterises Jesus as regularly going off alone, or with his disciples, to a mountain or to a deserted place to pray. All three of the Synoptic Gospels portray Jesus as undergoing a lengthy period of withdrawal immediately after his baptism:

'Then Jesus was led up by the Spirit into the wilderness to be tempted by the devil. He fasted for forty days and forty nights, and afterwards he was famished. The tempter came and said to him, "If you are the Son of God, command these stones to become loaves of bread." But he answered, "It is written,

'One does not live by bread alone,

but by every word that comes from the mouth of God'."

Then the devil took him to the holy city and placed him on the pinnacle of the temple, saying to him, "If you are the son of God, throw yourself down; for it is written,

'He will command his angels concerning you', and 'on their hands they will bear you up, so that you will not dash your foot against a stone'."

Jesus said to him, "again it is written,

'Do not put the Lord your God to the test'."

Again, the devil took him to a very high mountain and showed him all the kingdoms of the world and their splendour; and he said to him, "All these I will give you, if you will fall down and worship me". Jesus said to him, "Away with you, Satan! For it is written,

'Worship the Lord your God, and serve only him'."

Then the devil left him, and suddenly angels came and waited on him.'[4]

Mark, unlike Matthew or Luke, does not elaborate upon the exact nature of this experience of withdrawal: he simply states that Jesus was driven into the wilderness by the Spirit; that he was tempted by Satan; that he was with the wild beasts and that angels waited on him. Some have seen in the Matthaean and Lucan accounts not so much an historical account as a theological reflection on who Jesus is in the light of the Hebrew scriptures. Whatever the case may be two things may be said. First, that the tradition of faith understands Jesus to have undergone severe testing, as the Letter to the Hebrews indicates:

'We do not have a high priest who is unable to sympathise with our weaknesses, but we have one who in every respect has been tested as we are, yet without sin. Let us therefore approach the throne of grace with boldness, so that we may receive mercy and find grace to help in time of need.'[5]

It is possible to locate this experience of testing not only in the wilderness, but in the Garden of Gethsemane, for example, and supremely, of course, on the cross.

Secondly, that the suggestion that Jesus underwent an experience of testing during a period of solitary withdrawal rings true with our own spiritual experience, namely: that a profound experience of union with God also involves a confrontation with the self, and with darkness, and with all that is opposed to God in the light of that union.

It is significant that the wilderness experience follows on directly from the baptism. The desire for withdrawal was motivated by love, indeed it was at the inspiration of the Spirit that Jesus withdrew. The awareness of his Father's love made known in the Spirit at his baptism increased within him the desire to be alone and delight in that love. This is only to be expected. Where human relationships are concerned people in love enjoy being alone in order to let their love grow and flourish. Without such opportunities for withdrawal the love is likely to go cold. Withdrawal is an opportunity for love to be renewed at its source. The same applies in relation to God. We need periods of withdrawal to be renewed in God's love, to discover again the fundamental relationship in which we are grounded. The habit of setting aside time each day for prayer and meditation fulfils this purpose, as do more extended times of withdrawal and retreat.

The experience of love, though, can unsettle us, albeit in a creative and desirable way. We experience ourselves,

God and life differently, in ways which are not immediately understandable to us, and we need an opportunity to come to terms with the new awareness. This seems to be at the heart of Jesus' desire to withdraw into the desert. His baptism gave him a new awareness of his identity: as the Eternal Son forever coming from the Father in the Spirit of love, and forever returning to the Father in the Spirit of love. With this experience everything changed, and he needed time and space to work out all the implications of his newly-given awareness, to discover how to live his identity. To this end he withdrew into the desert.

We, too, may withdraw, either to rediscover God's love, or to work out the implications of a deeper experience of his love. Whatever the case it is not long before, within that very context, we are confronted with what seems to be the exact opposite. God as we have known him may disappear. We may be besieged with doubts or fears, with feelings of uncontrollable lust, anger or revenge, with boredom and apathy, with the awareness of failure in all sorts of areas of our lives and much else. It is in fact love which releases such things to the surface, the love of God which may be hidden to us, but which loosens them from their moorings deep in the unconscious. Such an experience can threaten, seemingly, to overwhelm and destroy us. Then we are tempted to do one or both of two things: either to run away from it, and pretend that it is not really part of us; or to give in to it and let it assume control of us. Either way we fail to cooperate with love's purpose, which is to allow all that is buried deep within us to come to the surface to be healed, transformed, and integrated, so that the space which it formerly occupied within us can now be filled with the love of God. It is only by becoming aware of all that seems to be opposed to God that we can surrender it to him for transformation. Much that is buried within us is there as a result of past hurts and fears, and it can be unnerving to have to face it, but only so do we emerge into the fullness of life in Christ, and we discover that what we are afraid of is nothing other than something which is really a perversion or distortion of its real nature.

Let us take just one example, that of sexuality. It may be most disconcerting to be overcome with thoughts and feelings that seem unacceptable to us, and the first inclination is to repress them. That is obviously what we have learnt to do in the past, though, imprisoning a part of us in fear and trepidation. The fact that we are becoming aware of them now undoubtedly increases our anxiety, but their emergence is due to love releasing them so that the energy which holds them in check can be channelled creatively as a part of who we are.

The second inclination, then, is to do the opposite of repressing them, it is to indulge them for all that they are worth. That which has kept them locked up has now been removed and the taste of freedom is exhilarating, and the wish to satisfy our longing is almost unstoppable. To do so, however, only leads to enslavement of a different kind. Now everything becomes subservient to the satisfaction of the desire, nothing is allowed to get in its way. The desire controls us, and we are just as imprisoned as we were when we repressed it.

The only other alternative is to let these feelings come into the full light of consciousness, neither judging or censoring them, nor indulging or satisfying them, but simply acknowledging and accepting them, being prepared to live with the pain and uncertainty which they cause. Gradually, within the love of God, they are transformed and redirected, so that our sexuality becomes the source of warmth and openness in our human relationships and with God, too. It becomes available to us as part of our giving and receiving love. Indeed it becomes available to God to enflesh his love within us, building all relationships up in the Spirit of love.

The temptation is always to settle for what promises to

lead to the fullness of life in the short term, but which, far from doing so actually takes us further away from real life by deceit. Whatever the totality of Jesus' experience of withdrawal may have been, it was something of which he was all too aware at every moment: the all-encompassing love of the Father in the Spirit; and the temptation to choose life away from that fundamental relationship. Jesus knew what it is like to be tempted and tested as we are. There is nothing wrong in temptation itself. It is usually the opportunity to grow into an even greater awareness of the fullness of life in the love of God. The test lies in resisting the temptation to settle for less than that abundance of life.

By being fully aware of what was within him Jesus was able to let all that potentially distorts and perverts to be used creatively. It was the total acceptance of himself that enabled him to be accepting of others, both in their creative and destructive capacities, and finally enabled him to accept the full force of evil that was unleashed upon him on the cross. The cross, another kind of withdrawal, was the fruit of his experience of withdrawal into the desert, for there is the full recognition and acceptance of all the destructive forces of evil, combined with an unwillingness to surrender to their power, and instead, their transformation into love, forgiveness and reconciliation.

It is the failure to acknowledge and accept the darker aspects of our experience, manifested either as repression or indulgence, which lends it the psychic power of evil, for evil is the powerful energy which emerges when anything is separated from God and centred on itself. Everything then becomes subservient to the one who is so separated, and the consequences can be horrific as history demonstrates. The battlefields of history are simply the unresolved battlefields of the heart.

At times withdrawal may appear to be either an unnecessary ordeal or a rather indulgent luxury. The truth of the matter is that it is only the withdrawal into our inmost selves in solitude and silence, usually enhanced by external withdrawal, which enables God to be given full entry into our lives, to transform us, and to lead us into the fullness of life in Christ.

CHAPTER SIX

Religionising

The Jews on me they made great suit,
And with me made great variance,
Because they loved darkness rather than light,
To call my true love to my dance:
Sing O my love, O my love, my love, my love;
This have I done for my true love.

Religion has always been an integral part of my life; it
could hardly have failed to be. My home from before I can
remember was a flat at the headquarters of a missionary
society in London, where my parents first met, and subsequently lived and worked. There was an endless succession
of visitors from all over the world who passed through our
doors.

Churchgoing was an important part of family life. My
earliest image of God was of an elderly, balding man,
dressed in green, standing far away. Only much later on
did I come to realise that this was our vicar wearing a
chasuble, whom I had obviously assumed to be God! I
sang in the church choir and the church was the centre of
my life, so much so that I would hold impromptu services
of my own at home, using sweets and cordial instead of
bread and wine!

It is somewhat amusing to have watched this habit pass
on to my own children. They have been rather more inven-
tive than ever I was, though. My eldest son, when still very
young, managed to have a set of stoles made for him to
suit his size! My second son regularly dressed up as a
bishop, and on one occasion went to the front door in his
episcopal clothes to discover the real bishop standing
there! My third son is the only one to have set up a perma-

nent altar in his bedroom! My daughter is above all this, and rarely has anything to do with it!

It was almost a foregone conclusion that I would be confirmed, and from the age of thirteen I became a regular communicant. Religion was an important feature of my school's life, and we were fortunate to have enterprising and stimulating chaplains, who devised imaginative services and preached well. During my final year something quite unexpected happened. I began to go into the Chapel late at night and pray. I would stay sometimes for an hour, and I felt irresistibly drawn to this practice. I thought that I began to discern the stirrings of a call to the religious life, but eventually it was felt more clearly to be a call to the priesthood. This precipitated a crisis: I was ready to proceed to university to read music, which now felt to me to be a mistake. Instead I thought that I should read theology. Common sense, but wise advice from one of the chaplains recommended that I continue as planned, and if the vocation was genuine it would stand the test of time.

My university years were fairly decadent spiritually. I hardly ever darkened the door of a church, except for a concert, or, out of habit, at home, the decision to do what was expected being easier than the opposite. Only later, when I was first married, did the desire to resume a regular association with a church return. Then the vocation made itself felt again, and the step towards ordination became smaller.

I have always loved the ceremonial and the music in church, and still do, and generally I rather enjoy the life of the Church. Precisely because of that the church is also a source of pain. Rather, it is not so much the church alone, as religion in general, for as well as being a tremendous force for good, it can also be at the same time a powerful manifestation of evil. Some of the worst things that have ever happened have been done in the name of one religion or another, and with their approval. It is scarcely surprising that many people are inhibited from becoming aware of God because of how they see his followers live and behave.

Sadly there is nothing new in this, although it is a salutary thought that the focus of conflict for Jesus was his own religion. The emergence of Jesus from out of the desert into Galilee after his period of withdrawal was like an explosion of life. Life erupted in an unprecedented way. The time spent in solitude was the prelude to an active expenditure of love such as the world had never known. Arising out of the knowledge of his Father's love came the desire for the whole creation to know itself to be part of that rhythm of love, too, dancing in the life of the Spirit. With love and compassion Jesus made himself completely available to the Father so that the Holy Spirit could be released through him, bringing people into the fullness of life. This was the very essence of Jesus' ministry. In St Luke's Gospel Jesus is portrayed as entering the synagogue in his home town, and identifying himself, with the words of the prophet Isaiah:

'The Spirit of the Lord is upon me, because he has anointed me to bring good news to the poor.

He has sent me to proclaim release to the captives, and recovery of sight to the blind, to let the oppressed go free, to proclaim the year of the Lord's favour.'[1]

In St John's Gospel Jesus summarised his purpose very simply:

'I came that they may have life, and have it abundantly.'[2]

The signs of life consisted mainly in healings. The whole Jewish people, of course, longed for liberation: their history had been one of oppression at the hands of one country or another, and at the time of Jesus' earthly life they were subjected to the Romans. Not surprisingly then, many looked for a messiah who would liberate them from tyranny and oppression in a temporal sense. During his period of withdrawal Jesus had no doubt considered that possibility as a way of realising his identity and vocation.

In the event he rejected it, and that is what would seem to lie behind the final temptation as it appears in St Matthew's Gospel:

'Again the devil took him to a very high mountain and showed him all the kingdoms of the world and their splendour; and he said to him, "all these I will give you if you will fall down and worship me." Jesus said to him, "Away with you, Satan! For it is written,

'Worship the Lord your God, and serve only him'."[3]

Had Jesus opted for this path life would never have been released in all its fullness; it would have been confined to the realisation of nationalistic aspirations. More importantly, too, perhaps, it would not have released religion from death into a living relationship with God. It was into their ultimate identity in God that people needed to be led, and by receiving life at the hands of Jesus longings which penetrated far deeper than temporal hopes were fulfilled. This is what brought him into direct conflict with the religion of his day, and its authorities.

It is impossible to read the gospels and not have a sense that the vast majority of Jesus' waking moments seemed to be given over to healing of one kind or another, and it was his gifts of healing which attracted others to him:

'Jesus went throughout Galilee, teaching in their synagogues and proclaiming the good news of the kingdom and curing every disease and every sickness among the people. So his fame spread throughout all Syria, and they brought to him all the sick, those who were afflicted with various diseases and pains, demoniacs, epileptics, and paralytics, and he cured them. And great crowds followed him from Galilee, the Decapolis, Jerusalem, Judea, and from beyond the Jordan.'[4]

Ordinary people flocked to Jesus to receive from him the life for which they had longed and which had been denied them. The very capacity to heal invited people to wonder just who he was, for in and through him they found themselves brought into a living relationship with

God, a truth to which the very conflict entered into with the religious authorities attests.

It is also impossible not to read the gospels and be aware that Jesus was in conflict with the religion of his day almost from the beginning. From the start the authorities were suspicious of him. The healing of the paralytic man in the synoptic gospels was the first occasion of concern for them.[5] Jesus perceived all too clearly that the man's health ultimately was to be seen in the context of his relationship with God. Hence when the man was laid before him he simply said:

'Son, your sins are forgiven.'[6]

This, however, was too much for the scribes, who commented:

'Why does this fellow speak in this way? It is blasphemy! Who can forgive sins but God alone?'[7]

Thus the gospels present us with the paradox, that those who had been excluded from a living relationship with God, the ordinary people of the day, found that in Jesus they were released into life; and those whose raison d'être was to guide people in their relationship with God, could not see in him the presence of the God whom they were supposed to know. Those who made on Jesus a 'great suit' were primarily the authorities and functionaries of religion, because, as Jesus revealed, 'they loved darkness rather than light'.

What began as a dispute over the eligibility to forgive sins extended into a full-blown confrontation with the whole religious tradition and practice as represented by the authorities of the day. It was not so much that religion itself was wrong; rather that its officials failed to appreciate what it was for. Jesus, after all, was an observant Jew himself; the tradition played an important role in leading him to the discovery of his deepest identity. For the religious authorities of the day religion had all but ceased to be a living tradition, leading beyond itself to the mystery and reality of God, and instead it had become an end in

itself. Rather than guiding people into a life-giving relationship with God, religion, in the hands of its officials,
had become a protection and a barrier against God.

Little by little the religious authorities were exposed and
unsettled by Jesus. The matter boiled down to an issue of
life and death: in Jesus life was bursting forth, whereas in
the hands of the religious authorities the spiritual tradition
was leading to death. What was unsettling about Jesus was
that he showed that it is only by dying that we receive the
fullness of life. The challenge to the authorities was indeed
to die, to go beyond the limitations of the tradition, and
discover in Jesus the embodiment of the mystery and life of
God to which the tradition was to bear witness. Instead
they clung on to the way of living death, and sought to rid
themselves of Jesus.

What was unnerving for the religious authorities was
that they were unable to control Jesus and authorise what
he was doing. Instead it was he, who by his very being,
called into question their authority. The life which was
mediated through him was indeed unstoppable and
uncontrollable. His sole desire was to release the life of
God into creation, and to free creation into that life. The
release of life was itself the evidence of his authority:

'When John heard in prison what the Messiah was
doing, he sent word by his disciples and said to him, "Are
you the one who is to come, or are we to wait for
another?" Jesus answered them, "Go and tell John what
you hear and see: the blind receive their sight, the lame
walk, the lepers are cleansed, the deaf hear, the dead are
raised, and the poor have good news brought to them.
And blessed is anyone who takes no offence at me".'[8]

So, too, when the authorities asked for a sign to
convince them of his authority, Jesus replied, mysteriously,
that the only sign to be given was that of Jonah, in other
words the mystery of life breaking through and beyond
death:

'Then some of the scribes and Pharisees said to him,

"Teacher, we wish to see a sign from you." But he answered them, "An evil and adulterous generation asks for a sign, but no sign will be given to it except the sign of the prophet Jonah. For just as Jonah was for three days and three nights in the belly of the sea monster, so for three days and three nights the Son of Man will be in the heart of the earth. The people of Nineveh will rise up at the judgement with this generation and condemn it, because they repented at the proclamation of Jonah, and see, something greater than Jonah is here!" '[9]

The mystery of life bursting forth from death is precisely what was revealed in the conflict between Jesus and the institutional authorities, and this is the deeper meaning that lies behind the accusations made against him in the gospels of Matthew and Mark:

'Now the chief priests and the whole council were looking for false testimony against Jesus so that they might put him to death, but they found none, though many false witnesses came forward. At last two came forward and said, "This fellow said, 'I am able to destroy the temple of God and to build it in three days'." The high priest stood up and said, "Have you no answer? What is it that they testify against you?" But Jesus was silent. Then the high priest said to him, "I put you under oath before the living God, tell us if you are the Messiah, the Son of God." Jesus said to him, "You have said so. But I tell you, from now on you will see the Son of Man seated at the right hand of Power and coming on the clouds of heaven."

Then the high priest tore his clothes and said, "He has blasphemed! Why do we still need witnesses? You have now heard his blasphemy. What is your verdict?" They answered, "He deserves death".'[10]

In a very real sense the tradition, represented by the temple and all that it stood for, had to be transcended. A religious institution is capable only of guiding us to the point where we realise that it has to be left behind if we are truly to enter into the fullness of life in God. The attempt to remove Jesus by death resulted only in proving his case, for the life which exploded through him at the beginning of his Galilean ministry broke out again, after the attempt to destroy it, in his resurrection, leading to the awareness that in Jesus 'something greater than the temple is here'.[11] If we are to enter into the fullness of life to which the religious tradition at best bears witness we have to enter into the mystery of death and resurrection, being prepared to let go of what seems most important of all, in order to discover the reality behind it and ultimately life itself. In the end nothing can confine God.

The religious authorities were not prepared to receive this truth. Instead of letting go of their security and passing beyond boundaries they failed to let God breathe life into the religious tradition and by contrast determined who God could be and what he could do in the light of their limited perception. Almost everything Jesus did was called into question: mixing with tax-collectors and sinners,[12] failing to observe regulations about fasting,[13] breaking the law of the Sabbath,[14] and failing to observe the rules concerning ritual ablutions.[15] As far as Jesus was concerned the authorities had failed to see that the whole purpose of religion was to lead to a living relationship with God. Instead they had allowed it to become an end in itself, and, in the process, had shielded themselves against God. No wonder that the words of the prophet Isaiah were perceived to be fulfilled in them:

'In vain do they worship me, teaching human precepts as doctrines.'[16]

The very purpose of religion was destroyed in its practice:

'You lock people out of the kingdom of heaven. For you do not go in yourselves, and when others are going in, you stop them.'[17]

It is tempting, of course, to assume that we are immune from such a conflict, that it was simply a matter between Jesus and the religious authorities of his day. This is far from being so, indeed the conflict manifests itself in every religion, in every generation and in every person, for in the end it is a simple issue of life or death. This awareness lies at the very heart of the Jewish religion itself:

'I call heaven and earth to witness against you today that I have set before you life and death, blessings and curses. Choose life so that you and your descendants may live, loving the Lord your God, obeying him, and holding fast to him.'[18]

The danger is always that we limit and confine life, even when we think that we are choosing it, and this is most obviously and disarmingly so in matters of religion. The authorities of Jesus' day had allowed matters of secondary, derivative importance so to occupy their attention, that they lost sight of the very core around which such things revolved. This is the truth revealed in an encounter between Jesus and a scribe, rare for its demonstration of agreement between them.[19] The scribe asked Jesus for his view as to which commandment was the most important. In response Jesus said that it was to love God, and, added, to love one's neighbour, too. This was breathtaking in its simplicity, for there were six hundred and thirteen precepts of the law, and the Pharisees had so concentrated on many of the lesser ones that they had lost sight of the essentials of which Jesus reminded them.

The pharisaic pattern is repeated time and time again, though. In every religion matters of secondary importance are exalted over and above the central truth and experience from which they derive. The mystery and reality of God becomes obscured by endless rules and regulations, tests of orthodoxy of one kind or another assume precedence over the invitation to love, and religion becomes tainted with death rather than imbued with life. It is not that codes of belief and practice are unnecessary, unimportant or dispensable; far from it. They are vital, and the religious traditions in which they are held are indispensable, for their purpose is to keep the mystery of God alive, and to be the channel through which his life is received. What goes wrong is that we fail to realise that God himself infinitely transcends them. Religion can bring us to the brink of mystery, but our nerve fails and rather than passing beyond into the mystery itself, we limit God to what we can cope with comfortably, where no more demands need to be made on us. In so doing we fail to enter into the fullness of life.

In addition to the scribe who asked Jesus the question about the law, there was one other official representative of the religion who demonstrated a humble openness to the essential mystery to which religion theoretically bears witness: Nicodemus. St John's Gospel portrays him as recognising the authority and authenticity of Jesus:

'Rabbi, we know that you are a teacher who has come from God; for no one can do these signs that you do apart from the presence of God.'[20]

In what follows Jesus seeks to demonstrate to Nicodemus that the reality of God can be truly known only by a break with what is known in favour of the unknown, a break as dramatic as leaving the womb of the mother in order to be born:

'Very truly, I tell you, no one can see the kingdom of God without being born from above ... what is born of the flesh is flesh, what is born of the Spirit is spirit.'[21]

The Spirit is beyond comprehension and control:

The wind blows where it chooses, and you hear the sound of it, but you do not know where it comes from or where it goes. So it is with everyone who is born of the Spirit.'[22]

Nicodemus was a teacher, a religious authority, and he was being led to the awareness that the mystery of God to which religion bears witness infinitely transcends religion itself. The purpose of religion is to reveal the mystery, but it only does so by pointing beyond itself. So all religious traditions bring us to the point where the religion itself has to be left behind, and the mystery which it reveals embraced. When we allow ourselves to do that a glorious awareness is born in us. Paradoxically we discover that in passing through and beyond all religious forms we find the mystery of God present in all religious traditions and in all people. By refusing to identify God with any partial reality we find all partial realities made whole in him.

What is it, then, that leads us to turn religion in on itself, and become the very thing that obscures the mystery and reality of God? It can only be the fear of truly coming alive. Religion can lead us to the loving God but it can also be used as a screen to shield us from the transcendent reality of God and therefore from life. There is security in dogma and ritual. The experience of the fullness of life, however, requires a willingness to die to what is known and enter into what is as yet unknown, and, at heart, we are afraid to die. Jesus revealed, though, that if we are prepared to die, the life of God is present beyond death, and is known in resurrection, indeed the fullness of life is known and received only through and beyond death. This is the essential truth and reality at the heart of everything. It is none other than the mystery of Christ himself.

CHAPTER SEVEN

Trusting

For thirty pence Judas me sold,
His covetousness to advance;
'Mark whom I kiss, the same do hold',
The same is he shall lead the dance:
Sing O my love, O my love, my love, my love;
This have I done for my true love.

My father always used to rise early. He would enjoy
having some time to himself. After completing some necessary tasks he would sit quietly, sometimes with a book and
a cup of tea, long before others were awake. Except me so
it seemed. From as early an age as I can remember I would
get up when I heard him and I would simply be with him,
often reading a book on my own, as he read his.

I suspect that it was this early experience among others
which contributed significantly to whatever capacity I
developed to trust. My father seemed completely reliable
and dependable. I have fond memories of sitting on the
pillion of his motorbike, my hands firmly around his waist
in front of me, completely confident that with him I was
safe.

It was he who taught me to swim. He was a good
swimmer himself, and swam frequently, and I have no
recollection that he ever lost patience with me as he encouraged me in the belief that all I had to do was swim. I
discovered how to swim by allowing my father to hold me
just below the surface of the water, and as I motioned with
my arms and legs so he would propel himself along the
pool with his hands under my tummy. As I grew in confidence so he would decrease the firmness of his hold on me,

until eventually he would let go, and I was left to swim unaided. At first I was unaware that he was no longer holding me, and it was in the moment of realising this that my nerve failed, and in thinking that I could not swim unaided, I found that my thoughts were confirmed to be correct!

It was not my father who taught me to ride a bicycle, but my cousin. One afternoon, quite unexpectedly, I found myself accompanying him somewhere to idle time away. We came to a long stretch of flat ground and he invited me to try the bicycle. Just as my father had held me in the swimming pool, so he held the bicycle upright and pushed gently, while I pedalled and learnt how to balance. It was not too long before the skill was learnt, and I enjoyed the sensation of travelling faster than I was able to on my feet. At one moment I asked if he would stop, but nothing happened. I turned around to discover that I had been cycling on my own, and that my cousin was far back in the distance. I had learnt to cycle without realising it, but in that moment of awareness I panicked and lost my balance.

Children seem to have an innate capacity to trust. Even when they are hurt and badly treated their ability to let go of themselves to another far exceeds what we should expect. What gets in the way of our trusting so often is our thinking: thinking that we are unable to do what is asked of us.

This was my experience on the only occasion when I have been ice-skating. Now I was no longer a child but an adult. It all looked so easy! I knew that as with so many other things, such as swimming and cycling, all that was necessary was to let it happen and not think about it, and yet for nearly the whole of the session I clung to the side of the ice-rink, not daring to let go of the side. The longer I stayed there, of course, the harder it became to venture out. My mind was telling me two contradictory things: first that everyone else was able to do it, and that all I had to do was let go; secondly, that it was very difficult, and that if I did try I would certainly fall down and hurt myself, and be humiliated in failure. As time moved on I became progressively more angry and frustrated, persuading myself and others that I did not really want to skate anyway. It was a profound delusion: I wished to skate with all my heart. I resented the fact that it seemed to be so easy for everyone else, and became irritated by the frequent assurances from others that there was nothing to it. With barely more than a few minutes left before the session closed I galvanised all my strength and asked two teenagers if they would take my hands and guide me out on to the ice. With my heart racing in trepidation I allowed myself to be led out into freedom. It would be wrong to say that it was the most wildly successful thing that I had ever done: I slipped over frequently, but I soon learned that the falling was not nearly so bad as I had expected, and moreover, that it was possible, more often than to slip, to remain upright, and enjoy living in a quite new and different world.

It is a rare treat to find someone who is completely trusting. Most of us have grown up with a mixture of trust and fear, and yet we know that the most exhilarating and fulfilling moments of our lives are to be enjoyed when we allow ourselves to be drawn out beyond our limited horizons and experience into an ever greater fullness of life. What is called falling in love is the most obvious example. The love of another awakens within us the desire to respond, but the fullness of love is not known until we give ourselves in trust to the other, to discover that they do the same thing towards us, and that in that mutual giving and receiving of love there is complete security. The willingness to give ourselves away in trust is the key to entering into life.

Many, however, are profoundly damaged in their capacity to trust. From childhood onwards people suffer the denial or the disappearance of love and affection, or its more positive absence, as it were, in terms of cruelty, abuse and violence. They discover that they cannot entrust their well-being to those closest to them, and they develop a profound suspicion towards others and to life in general. As a result of such experience they often grow up with a lack of confidence in themselves, too, believing that what has happened to them has somehow or other been their fault, that they do not deserve the trust of others. Even in such people, however, there is nearly always the desire to trust, the longing to give themselves to another in response to the love which they may have for them, and the hope that one day their deepest longings will be fulfilled.

All of us, though, whether badly wounded in our ability to trust or not, find it difficult to trust come what may as a fundamental response to life. We fear that we are not wise to let go of ourselves completely, and in so doing enter into the fullness of life. The result is that we find ourselves hiding from our desire to give ourselves away in trust for fear of being rejected, for fear of failing, for fear of being proved wrong after all, and we look for satisfaction in less demanding ways, or even distorted ways. Yet in all people this desire to give in trust, in however perverted a way it may find expression, is ultimately a response to the prior giving in trust of another in the depths of our being: God himself.

The impulse to give ourselves away in trust is in fact grounded in God. Some people are aware of this from an early age; in others it is obscured for various reasons. In all, though, his presence is a mystery, hidden, yet made known to us as we respond in trust, and leave what is known and venture towards the unknown. Our awareness of God increases in the proportion to which we are prepared to leave our security behind, and give ourselves away in trust to what as yet remains mysteriously hidden, and yet which beckons us out of ourselves. It is only in trust that we can know God:

'By faith Abraham obeyed when he was called to set out

for a place that he was to receive as an inheritance; and he set out, not knowing where he was going.'[1]

Such a call is received within ourselves. It is in fact an intimation of the fullness of truth into which we are being drawn: that in the depths of our being there is a movement, a rhythm, a dance of love, in which we are being invited to participate, and which we can only know if we give ourselves to it. The giving is an act of trust.

The call which is uttered deep within us is made known in Jesus himself. He summons us to give ourselves in trust to him, and to follow, and in so doing find that our self-giving is reciprocated at the deepest level of all. It is in fact an invitation to entrust ourselves to him for life itself. In all of the gospels Jesus is portrayed as calling others to be with him from the very beginning of his Galilean ministry:

'As Jesus passed along the Sea of Galilee, he saw Simon and his brother Andrew casting a net into the lake – for they were fishermen. And Jesus said to them, "Follow me, and I will make you fish for people." And immediately they left their nets and followed him. As he went a little farther, he saw James, son of Zebedee and his brother John, who were in their boat mending the nets. Immediately he called them; and they left their father Zebedee in the boat with the hired men, and followed him.'[2]

We are not given all the biographical details of those who were called. The impression given, however, is that the response was immediate. Without question they simply left what they were doing and gave themselves to Jesus in trust. It cannot be claimed that it is always quite like that for us, or for most other people either. The response is usually gradual, and we realise that the call has been uttered over a long period of time, but that we have failed to notice it. Furthermore the call never ceases: the invitation to give in trust continues at every moment, just as it does in human relationships. Indeed there are times when in the context of a relationship, human or divine, the call invites an increasingly deeper response, a more complete giving of the self, at which we baulk. We believe that we are unable to entrust ourselves that much. Yet, although we sometimes fail, we also find that we are capable of what is required as well.

The significant thing about the call is that it is sheer grace. It is not of our own making, nor do we expect it, in fact the harder we try to look for a call the further the possibility seems to recede of our discerning it. It is obscure and hidden, and it catches unawares. We do nothing to warrant it, it is simply there. In that call we know that we are loved and valued and wanted. This call is present within the whole of creation, and is uttered in the Son in eternity. The true nature of this utterance is disclosed in Jesus, and the Spirit within us enables us to respond, by giving ourselves in trust to him, who leads us to the one who utters the call, the Father. To respond to the call is to realise the truth of our being: it is our vocation to find ourselves as part of the dance of love. Among those who have responded to this utterance of love, and to the invitation to find its fulfilment by the giving of the self in trust to Jesus, is Judas Iscariot, 'who betrayed him'.[3]

Tradition encourages us to see in Judas someone who was thoroughly reprehensible and beyond hope, singled out in this respect from all others. Such a judgement, however, would seem to be unfair and even undeserved. It is important that we try to understand Judas in the total context, because he is important to us.

First of all it has to be acknowledged that, unlike many others, he did initially respond. There was in Judas a capacity to give himself in trust, and in Jesus he saw one who met his desires and needs. The gospels bear witness to the fact that not everyone was able so to entrust themselves to Jesus, the most well-known of which, perhaps, being the Rich Young Man. He clearly responded to something in Jesus, for he came to ask him about eternal life. He found it difficult, so it would seem, though, to respond completely:

'Jesus said to him, "If you wish to be perfect, go, sell your possessions and give the money to the poor, and you will have treasure in heaven; then come, follow me". When the young man heard this word he went away grieving for he had many possessions.'[4]

Secondly, Judas was not alone, in wondering whether the hope of the fullness of life glimpsed in response to Jesus might not after all have been a mistake. Certainly that was how it began to appear. With Jesus came two related developments. First there was an explosion of life, love and grace to which many people responded whole-heartedly. In all kinds of ways they entrusted themselves to him, and, as a result, were released into a new dimension of life. Secondly, at exactly the same time, there was a corresponding response to suppress that life, indeed the two impulses were set for a head-on collision. The progression towards that denouement raised, in almost all associated with Jesus, doubts about whether they had been wise to entrust themselves to him, as is suggested by the fact that when it did finally came about, only a handful of people remained constant. Not even Peter, who had failed fully to understand Jesus, but had protested that he would die with him if necessary, was able to hold his nerve, and while Jesus' trial was taking place he denied that he had ever had anything to do with him. It must have looked as though their own trust in Jesus had been misplaced.

Judas stands out in this context, not as the only one whose nerve failed, but as the one whose nerve failed the most. It is hard to discern his motives completely. The gospels record that he betrayed Jesus for money. St. John's gospel implies that Judas was not to be trusted anyway. In the incident where Jesus was anointed at Bethany Judas asked why the money spent on the perfume had not been sold and given to the poor. The evangelist explains what lay behind his question:

'He said this not because he cared about the poor but

because he was a thief; he kept the common purse and used to steal what was put into it.'[5]

This may well seem to attribute to Judas a thoroughly base motive, but we know from our own experience that human personalities with their complexes, drives and instincts are rarely so uncomplicated. When Judas first responded to the call of Jesus he was no different from anyone else in not yet being a whole person, indeed it was precisely to such people that Jesus had come:

'Those who are well have no need of a physician, but those who are sick; I have come to call not the righteous but sinners.'[6]

Furthermore, it is impossible to render Judas wholly responsible for Jesus' death. We might well conclude that even without Judas' act of betrayal Jesus would still have been eliminated. There were many opportunities for the authorities to arrest him, and, indeed, on other occasions, were minded to do so:

'The Pharisees heard the crowd muttering such things about him, and the chief priests and Pharisees sent temple police to arrest him.'[7]

It would seem difficult, then, to look at Judas in so straightforward a manner. Something much more subtle must have been at work. For some reason or other Judas found himself distancing himself from Jesus. The breakdown of relationships rarely happens just like that, even if it appears to be so. More often than not something small begins to irritate and builds up over the course of time. Eventually inadequacies and grievances are looked for, until the accumulated effect causes a major, unbridgeable rift. Resentment and hurt block the way to reconciliation.

We have no way of knowing what passed between Jesus and Judas in this respect. It would not be unreasonable to assume, though, that whatever relationship there had been had been breaking down over a period of time. For some reason or other Judas no longer saw in Jesus the one who could lead to the fulfilment of his deepest desires. It may have been disappointment in him, or fear. If we are to accept that Judas was no less complicated than the rest of us, though, we should surely not be wrong to believe that Judas was not motivated by the sole desire for money. Much more likely would it be that when he found himself under pressure, with potential demands being made on him by his continued association with Jesus, he resorted to the apparent security of something far less valuable. His propensity for theft would suggest that in part he was a taker rather than a giver in his general attitude to life, and we have no idea what might have contributed to this weakness. As with all of us there will have been influences from the past which will have encouraged him to preserve his life, and insulate himself against hurt by taking rather than by giving and trusting. His continued association with Jesus almost certainly brought to the surface profound anxieties and insecurities, which could only be coped with by providing security in another way: money.

It may seem absurd to us to think that Judas could have believed that thirty pieces of silver would have been the answer to his problems, but then we look for solutions to our difficulties in the most ridiculous ways. We turn to drugs, alcohol, sex, power, wealth, reputation and a whole host of other things for comfort. Even when we are aware of our weakness, and try to do something about it, it is invariably the case that when pressures mount we turn to them once again. So the alcoholic who has been dry for months reaches the point when, under severe pressure, a single drink offers the promise of salvation. The sexual abuser re-offends; and so on. Judas' weakness was money. His security against uncertainty was something as simple as that, and if in Jesus he had found someone who seemed to offer something more secure, a point was clearly reached when, consciously or not, Judas concluded that what Jesus had promised was not going to be delivered. In the mounting conflict the future with Jesus looked decidedly insecure, and Judas resorted to his weakness.

The act of betrayal, therefore, was the outward manifestation of something profoundly complex going on within him. He had already betrayed, or was in the process of betraying, his deepest self, which had come to life in response to Jesus, to a lesser self, and his deal with the authorities was the external unravelling of this truth.

The death of Jesus would almost certainly have come about without Judas, so what is it that singles him out in the whole drama? It is not so much the act of betrayal, terrible though that was, but his suicide. As the full burden of self-knowledge came to light, as a result of the events that unfolded before him, Judas could not live with it. He could no longer give himself in trust to Jesus; he could give himself in trust to nothing and no one, not even himself. Of all those in the drama he was the only one who reached this point. Others died with Jesus, but no one else took their own life. The fullness of life which had burst forth in Jesus, and which had been awakened in Judas, was rejected. Judas found himself in terrible isolation, completely enclosed within himself, and he could not bear it. Money offered no security against hell. The only hint of relief lay in death:

'When Judas, his betrayer, saw that Jesus was condemned, he repented and brought back the thirty pieces of silver to the chief priests and the elders. He said, "I have sinned by betraying innocent blood." But they said, "What is that to us? See to it yourself." Throwing down the pieces of silver in the Temple, he departed; and he went and hanged himself.'[8]

Judas was not the only one who came to regret his own actions. Peter did, too. After his denial of Jesus he, too, was burdened with painful self-knowledge:

'Then Peter remembered what Jesus had said:

"Before the cock crows, you will deny me three times."
And he went out and wept bitterly.'[9]

What singles Judas out as much as anything else is his
death. And the manner of his dying is in marked contrast
to that of Jesus.

There are some circumstances in which I could imagine
contemplating suicide: a moral lapse that brought shame
upon myself and my family or the Church; the prospect of
indescribable suffering and torture; a future with no hint
of meaning, purpose or value. It is possible to envisage
reaching a stage when the desire to give oneself in trust,
the will to live at all, simply disappeared. There are many
who have reached that point, and continue to do so. The
death of Jesus was for those who reach this point, too,
which is why Judas is so important to us.

We cannot imagine that Jesus looked forward to
the inevitable outcome of the conflict with any relish. If
the future looked insecure and unknown, since death in
the sense that he was about to undergo it had never been
experienced before, then the only certainty lay in the
knowledge that its manner would be cruel and torturous.
It is hardly surprising, therefore that he hoped that it could
be avoided. Moreover he flinched from the prospect of
death:

' "I am deeply grieved, even to death; remain here and
stay awake with me". And going a little farther, he threw
himself on the ground and prayed, "My Father, if it is
possible, let this cup pass from me".'[10]

St. Luke characterises the ordeal even more strongly:

'In his anguish he prayed more earnestly, and his sweat
became like great drops of blood falling down on the
ground.'[11]

The experience of Jesus was almost identical to that of
Judas. Both found themselves under extreme pressure in
the light of circumstances, and both questioned the
assumptions on which their lives had been based. We
cannot assume that Jesus' anguish was caused only by the

prospect of physical pain. He must also have been subjected to intense doubt, too, about whether he might not have been deluded also. Venturing into the unknown is always accompanied by an element of doubt. Jesus was faced, therefore, with a choice: either renounce everything that he believed in and lived by, and thereby sell his soul, as Judas had done; or hold on to everything that he stood for and as a result lose everything, even the assurance that he was right to do so. It was a situation in which it appeared that he could not win.

As the pressure worked one way for Judas, so it worked the other way for Jesus. He had lived his whole life in trust. The relationship with the Father was the all-embracing reality in which he lived, and which he sought to share with others. This relationship was something into which he grew, though: in his human consciousness he had to become aware, gradually, of his divine identity, which was revealed at his baptism. The manner of Jesus' awareness of his Father can have been no different from that of any other person, though. There was no other route to this knowledge than the awareness of a hidden presence within the depths of his being, gradually making itself felt. The only way in which he could know the true nature of that presence was by giving himself in trust to it. As he did so he discovered it to be a personal love, transcending everything, known only by leaving behind everything that was already known and familiar, and entrusting himself to what lay beyond, as yet unknown.

The same is true for all. We can only know God by entrusting ourselves to him, and what beckons us within is a luminous darkness. God is present within us, and yet always beyond us, and we realise the presence of God by giving ourselves away in trust, in fact by dying.

Jesus sought to communicate the awareness of God by suggestion, seeking to capture its elusive, hidden nature:

' "The kingdom of heaven is like treasure hidden in a

field, which someone found and hid; then in his joy he goes and sells all that he has and buys that field."

"Again, the kingdom of heaven is like a merchant in search of fine pearls. On finding one pearl of great value, he went and sold all that he had and bought it".[12]

He knew better than anyone else that to live in the love of the Father was to make a continuous gift of the self in trust into a presence that was always beyond. Life is released only in the act of dying.

As the conflict came to a head the pressure mounted on Jesus to conclude whether this was the truth by which he lived or not. Here was the ultimate experience of death, the real unknown, into which he was being called and beckoned. At this point Jesus continued to live as he had always done, by giving himself to the Father in complete trust:

'Yet not what I want but what you want.'[13]

The test that had faced him in the desert after his baptism occurred again at its most intense here. The battle won in the desert was the foundation of triumph in Gethsemane.

We cannot underestimate the significance of Jesus' gift of himself to the Father in complete trust. Without it the resurrection could not have been revealed. The life which was released through Jesus as he emerged from the desert into Galilee was the same life which was released in resurrection, and which had brought creation into being in the first place. Had Jesus refused to give himself in Gethsemane, though, life would never have been known to burst through the ultimate unknown, and the true nature of God would have remained undisclosed.

Judas, of course, could not have known of the triumph of life through and beyond death. Jesus did not know it for certain. He only knew it in an act of total trust. What was revealed in him, though, was not for him alone. It was for the whole of creation, to demonstrate that the life of God cannot be destroyed, that it always waits for us, to be given and received in trust. Jesus' death was for Judas, and for all those who cannot give themselves in trust any longer, that love and life might continue to dance in them when they cannot even see it or believe in it any more.

CHAPTER EIGHT

Suffering

Before Pilate the Jews me brought,
Where Barrabbas had deliverance;
They scourged me and set me at nought,
Judged me to die to lead the dance:
Sing O my love, O my love, my love, my love;
This have I done for my true love.

The fact that Jesus gave himself in trust to his Father in
that crucial moment in Gethsemane does not in any way
seem to minimise the horror we feel when we contemplate
what that decision entailed for him. His suffering is almost
too awful to behold, and we flinch from it in the depths of
our being. From the moment that he arose from his knees
he was gradually stripped and deprived of practically
everything that we consider to belong to the dignity of a
human being. He was the object of misunderstanding,
ridicule, cruelty and sheer evil. First he became the play-
thing of two groups of people, beginning with members of
the Jewish Council itself:

'Then the high priest tore his clothes and said, "Why do
we still need witnesses? You have heard his blasphemy!
What is your decision?" All of them condemned him as
deserving death. Some began to spit on him, to blindfold
him, and to strike him, saying to him, "Prophesy!" The
guards also took him over and beat him.'[1]

Following the audience with Pilate, too, he was passed
into the hands of the soldiers:

'Then the soldiers led him into the courtyard of the
palace (that is, the governor's headquarters); and they
called together the whole cohort. And they clothed him in

a purple cloak; and after twisting some thorns into a crown, they put it on him. And they began saluting him, "Hail, King of the Jews!" They struck his head with a reed, spat upon him, and knelt down in homage to him. After mocking him, they stripped him of the purple cloak and put his own clothes on him. Then they led him out to crucify him.'[2]

By now his body had been violated and no consideration whatsoever was given to his feelings. He was subjected to the wholly understandable fear and apprehension in the face of raw and intimidating cruelty. It was not over yet, though. As he hung on the cross, tortured by pain of an almost unimaginable intensity, he was humiliated by the jeers of the crowd. Even his companions in death, from whom he might reasonably have expected a degree of compassion in the selfsame circumstances, taunted him:

'Those who passed by derided him, shaking their heads and saying, "Aha! You who would destroy the temple and build it in three days, save yourself, and come down from the cross!" In the same way the chief priests, along with the scribes, were also mocking him among themselves and saying: "He saved others; he cannot save himself. Let the Messiah, the King of Israel, come down from the cross now, so that we may see and believe." Those who were crucified with him also taunted him.'[3]

Finally, in addition to all the other pain came spiritual pain, the worst of all, as he was deprived even of the awareness of the Father:

'At three o'clock Jesus cried out with a loud voice, "Eloi, Eloi, Lema Sabachthani?" which means, "My God, my God, why have you forsaken me?" '[4]

In this experience of suffering Jesus was reduced to nothing, 'set at nought'; and as we look at him in his suffering, so, too, are we. There is something about it which makes our minds baulk. In order to understand it we have, literally, to 'stand under' it, to know and feel its weight, its horror, its awfulness. Yet everything within us protests. The desire to make sense of it is so strong, and yet we know that in order to do so we have to receive from it what it wishes to give, and we perceive that its only 'gift' is destruction and disintegration. We fear that as soon as we begin to accommodate it just a little it is but a short route to opening ourselves to the forces of destruction on a vast scale. If we begin to make sense of this, so we persuade ourselves, we shall have to make sense of, and in making sense of, accept, a whole dimension of experience, which seems to be utterly and totally senseless: the totality of the accumulated pain and suffering of the universe as expressed in the mindless extermination of six million Jews, for example, the child abused and murdered, the person whose death is a direct result of the irresponsibility of a drunken driver, the shrunken figure who lies helpless and at the mercy of a ravaging, incurable disease; and so much more. To accept all this is to open ourselves to the reality of suffering in our own lives, and we are no different from Jesus in praying with our whole being that if possible the cup of suffering might pass us by. Suffering, we sense, is to be resisted.

Not only do we have more than a sneaking suspicion, though, that suffering is an inevitable part of all our experience. We also know that it is in the suffering of Jesus that we are drawn into the very mystery and reality of Christ, and that if we are truly to enter into life, and union with God, then we cannot skirt around it. Furthermore, there are others, most notably St. Paul, who almost rejoice in suffering, provided that it can be the means of union with Christ:

'I want to know Christ and the power of his resurrection and the sharing of his sufferings by becoming like him in his death, if somehow I may attain the resurrection from the dead.'[5]

At this point St Paul attracts and repels at the same time. The attraction lies in the confidence he expresses that being united with Christ in suffering is actually the path to glory:

'If we have been united with him in a death like his, we will certainly be united with him in a resurrection like his.'[6]

Here, we think, if all that is destructive and apparently negative in our experience can actually contribute to something more wonderful and creative than we can hardly envisage, then there is reason indeed for hope, confidence and rejoicing. We can open ourselves to the reality of suffering, and with St Paul, accept the loss of everything for the sake of knowing Christ, whose value surpasses everything else.

The repulsion lies in the fact that to contemplate the 'benefits' of suffering seems to involve a trivialisation of its horror. Not only is there a great deal of suffering in the world; so much of it seems to be devoid of any hope or purpose at all. To speak of the creativity, or of the redemptiveness of suffering, threatens to invite the accusation: if this were your experience, if this were your suffering, you would not even think of speaking so glibly.

So we find ourselves on the horns of a dilemma: unless we share in suffering we cannot enter fully into the mystery, reality and life of Christ. Yet to speak of the creative possibilities inherent in suffering runs the risk of riding roughshod over the sensitivities of others. We are indeed treading on holy ground. St Paul's authority for speaking of suffering lay in his own experience of it. It is perhaps true for us, too, that it is only on that same basis that we dare to speak of it.

There is a large part of me that wishes to reject the use of the word suffering to describe my experience. When I consider what others go through in one way and another I am aware that I could hardly bear to endure what they do. It is true for all of us, though, that there are times when our own pain, whatever its cause, is felt to be so great, that we know that we are indeed united with others in a shared bond of experience. Circumstances differ, but the intensity is recognisably the same, and suffering is known as something which threatens our life and well-being to the core, with little prospect of release or relief. It was an experience of illness which focused for me the reality of suffering.

I had never been seriously ill before, indeed I had never even been admitted to hospital. Within the period of two years or so which preceded the experience which I am about to describe, though, I had never before had so many viral infections, either. What began to emerge at this point, however, seemed to be more serious than a viral infection. I began to experience pains in my groin and my testes. At first I ignored them, thinking them to be of little consequence, but when they continued for three weeks or so I realised that I could no longer turn a blind eye to them. My wife persuaded me to visit the doctor, which I did. As I described the symptoms to him I could tell from his response that he was treating the matter with the utmost seriousness. He thought that I probably had an infection of the testes, prescribed antibiotics, and arranged for me to have an ultrasound scan test, in his words, 'to eliminate the possibility that it might be anything more serious'. He was concerned that I should not have the scan too soon lest it should show up an infection, which might itself have hidden something else. The antibiotics had to be given time to see if they could deal with the matter.

At this stage it did not really occur to me that there might be anything seriously wrong. In fact two or three days after seeing the doctor, and having started the course of antibiotics, I began to feel rather better. I felt that I could probably resume work fairly easily, and I very much wanted to be on my feet for a big diocesan service at church on the eve of Advent Sunday. Ironically it was a healing service! It lasted a great length of time, and in spite of the fact that we have a regular healing service each month in the church, I could not recall a time when I had felt so disinclined to have anything to do with healing! At the end I felt quite dreadful, and colleagues persuaded me to go home to bed.

The physical pain began to worsen. At times I would experience a burning sensation shooting down my legs, causing sleepless nights. The physical pain was the precursor of a period of spiritual darkness. The lack of any improvement caused overwhelming anxiety and I began to wonder whether there might not be something seriously wrong. Inevitably it began to occur to me that I might have something life-threatening such as cancer. Together with this were feelings of anger and guilt, and the most profound sense of failure, a sense that I had let others down. I found myself crying frequently, often moved by the most unexpected thing.

At the same time, though, I was aware of the words 'follow me', which seemed to be spoken in the depths of my being. I perceived it to be a call not to hide or run away from the experience. It also seemed to be an affirmation by God that I was loved, and that whatever the outcome of the illness, everything was, and would be, all right, even if it turned out that I was terminally ill.

More often than not this awareness was at best a background one, at worst only barely remembered. Most of the time I was worried and anxious, and I knew that others were, too. Simply not recovering was the greatest anxiety, and I wanted, somehow, to force the pace. I became painfully aware that the more effort I put into getting better the worse I became. Little by little I had to accept my helplessness and powerlessness. The doctor still believed that I had a viral infection and prescribed more antibiotics and painkillers, which seemed to have little or no effect. The possibility of a hospital admission began to be considered. I did not wish to come to this conclusion but it gradually began to dawn on me that perhaps God might be saying something to me in all this, and that what was being communicated was directly related to my immobility, my powerlessness, my inability to do anything, so it seemed, in my own strength.

I had been in bed for about three weeks, and at times I wondered if I would ever leave it. A glimmer of hope came from an unexpected direction. There is in my family an hereditary illness called 'Huntington's Disease'. It is a horrible disease, whose symptoms are the gradual loss of all faculties due to the progressive shrinking of the brain. An aunt and two cousins had already died as a result of it. The spectre of the illness hovered over the whole family. My aunt, my mother's sister, began to show signs of the disease when I was still very young. She was permanently resident in a hospital but occasionally enjoyed a visit to my grandparents' home. We would invariably join them on these fairly infrequent visits. My abiding memory is of someone who seemed to me at the time to be a monster. Limbs were uncontrollable, speech had degenerated into a series of grunts, and the whole person seemed to be wild. With the passage of time memory plays tricks, and I cannot remember now whether I did cower under the table, or whether I simply longed to do so. To be in her presence was too frightening and difficult for me to bear. Even at so young an age I could not understand how my father and grandfather could show so little anxiety and carry her in their arms. Only later did I come to know, of course, that it was due to love.

My cousins began to show the tell-tale signs of the disease when I was a teenager. Like her mother, Ann was eventually admitted to hospital, and restricted to a padded cell. Visits to her, rare though they were, were compounded by an intense anxiety about how to cope with her, together with a terrible guilt that in her suffering there was so little that I or anyone else seemed able to do. Communication seemed almost impossible, and it seemed to me that the degeneration of her personality imprisoned within her the essential part of her which was unreachable, consigning her to a hell of isolation which was truly awful.

In truth, of course, none of us can know for certain just how it is for the sufferer, but that is what I felt at the time.

The prospect of the illness being transmitted through my own immediate family seemed inevitable. At the age of sixteen my sister began to exhibit what we assumed to be symptoms. She complained of pains in her arms and legs, and I remember plucking up the courage on one occasion to ask my mother if she had got what Ann had. It must have been an awful moment for her, to have her unspoken fears articulated. Indeed I know that from the time of our birth my parents feared the emergence of symptoms. The illness hung over us like the Sword of Damocles.

It was not until I was eighteen that it was revealed that the illness could not possibly be transmitted through our side of the family A chance conversation between my mother and her aunt disclosed what my mother had never known: that her sister was in fact a half-sister, not my grandfather's daughter after all, and it was through my aunt's father that the illness had been passed.

As I lay ill in bed I found that I was thinking about my aunt and two cousins a great deal. I knew that I could not possibly have the illness, and I thought that I had dealt with my feelings about it all long before, but as I lay helpless and afraid it began to dawn on me that although I knew consciously that I could not contract the illness, unconsciously I had been expecting it, or at least I was living with the expectation that something dreadful would happen to me, and before I had lived an expected span of years. I began to see that my response to the slightest illness throughout my life had been a two-fold one: expecting the worst; and trying desperately hard not to succumb to illness, lest my worst fears be confirmed. I began to see how unconsciously at least, I had lived at a ridiculous pace, because deep down I had been expecting to die young, and in living with that attitude and at that pace I had in fact been putting an untenable pressure on my whole system, and that in trying to force the pace I was in fact running away: from God and from my true self.

This awareness dawned gradually, but with startling clarity. I felt that I had been seen through, that along with the legendary emperor not so much my new clothes, but my clothes of a lifetime had been shown to be little more than a figment of my imagination. I looked back on my whole life, on everything that I had been and done, and saw emptiness and shallowness. It seemed as though everything on which my life had been built had been demolished. My priesthood felt like a complete sham, and I wondered how I could ever face anybody again. I had the strongest suspicion that everybody else must have been able to see the truth, except me. Here was a liberating and terrifying truth: liberating, because so much of my life experience now began to make sense, and there was the possibility of living in a new way; terrifying, because the new way of life was only possible if the old were allowed to die, and letting the old die had to precede the emergence of whatever might follow. My identity was bound up with so much of the past, and without it I wondered what of 'me' would continue to exist.

I was faced with a simple choice: either to accept death in this form and trust that life would emerge somehow, or to avoid it, knowing that such a decision would indeed eventually kill me. The moment of acceptance was an act of surrender to God, whose presence I could barely sense now. Accepting the truth meant relinquishing a struggle which was gradually destroying me. The immediate consequence of doing so was that the physical symptoms of my illness began to disappear and deep within me I knew that the ultrasound scan test would not reveal the presence of anything unwelcome, which was indeed how it turned out to be.

The second, and far more significant result, was that in consenting to the death of part of myself, I was given an awareness of God such as I had never had before with such intensity. In the silent depths of my own being I knew myself again to be grounded in God, in whom my ultimate identity and being was found. Stripped of everything, so it seemed, on which my life had been built, I discovered afresh and more profoundly the reality of God beyond all. Here, now, was peace, stillness, healing and love of such quality, that I found it almost impossible to separate such things from the way in which they had been given to me: through suffering.

To put it thus is to speak of the redemptive power of suffering, the sense that it is not wasted, and can contribute to our ultimate well-being and completion in God, indeed, that God is present in and through suffering. This is undoubtedly so. The difficulty attendant upon this awareness, though, is that we have such a strong sense of the creative possibilities of suffering that we risk minimising its terror. Furthermore we can come very close to suggesting that God actually ordains suffering without any qualification at all, and we find ourselves having to say that because suffering can be creative then it is the will of God in all circumstances; and since God is love then suffering is a sign of his love, and we are then but a very short step form persuading ourselves that evil is in fact good. It is true, of course, that from within the awareness of God suffering can be seen in a different light, it can be creative and redemptive, but there are subtleties and nuances which have to be appreciated if we are to understand how it can be so. In this respect the task is not so different from the attempt to understand the precise nature of creation itself earlier, where a straight identification of God and creation was not permissible, although we had to affirm a strong sense of participation of each in the other. So, too, where suffering is concerned God and creation participate in each other in and through it, but not in such a way that God can be identified wholly with evil. We need to look clearly if we are truly to understand our own suffering, and that of Jesus, too.

I have to admit, first of all, that my own experience of being 'set at nought' was partly of my own making. Clearly I carried a great deal within me which was not my own fault, and in many ways I had tried to deal with this before the illness, but to say that I was wholly a victim would be inaccurate. The effect of an hereditary illness in the family was considerable, but I could not explain every inappropriate thought, intention and action of my life as stemming from this. Although I know myself to be bound in some measure, I also know what it is to exercise genuine freedom and choice. There had been warning signs before that I could not live at so fast a pace and expect to survive unharmed but I had taken little notice of them. Nor is it so that after the experience of illness my capacity to choose only the good has been perfected. I know that in many ways I still act selfishly and unlovingly, which cannot any longer be linked in any way to the fear of contracting an hereditary disease. Rather the illness was in part the consequence of choosing to live in a manner which was not consistent with God's purpose for me. At the most fundamental level I had chosen, in all sorts of ways throughout my life, to live without reference to God, thus separating myself from my life source, and indeed from my true self. There was also a part of me that clearly had chosen God, so that there was within me a division at the deepest level of my being, with the two parts of me fighting each other for supremacy. Such a struggle was bound to manifest itself in one way or another eventually, and my illness was the external way in which the internal division was brought to light.

This is a way of saying that suffering is partly the consequence of our own choices and actions. It results from choosing self exclusively rather than God and neighbour, too, and the inner law of our being is that if we continue to choose against the truth of God and of ourselves, we shall eventually be brought to see the result. This, then, is the equivalent to the function of pain at a physical level, as a means of warning us against certain choices and actions. The heat of the fire warns us that if we hold our hand in it for long our hand will be harmed. The pain alerts us to the harmful effects it may have if wrongly used. So, too, with suffering at the deepest level. As we are brought face to face with the consequences of how we have lived so we are given the opportunity to learn from the harmful effects of our choices. Suffering can teach. What it teaches most is that God is the fundamental reality, in whom we and all things are grounded, and if we ignore this truth we violate our own being, too. This is why the experience of suffering can, at the same time, lead to a profound awareness of God. He allows us to discover that he is everything, that we are to depend on him alone, and so in being stripped and 'set at nought' barriers to his presence are removed. For as long as we attempt to exclude him we experience only intense pressure within. All our energy is being used to keep at bay that which is far greater than we are. In the moment that we consent to the removal of all that obstructs God, God is able to enter into that space, which is his rightful home. In this light it is easy for us to see, then, how it is possible for us to be aware of the presence of God so close to where he is all but negated. It is at the very moment when things go wrong, when our world falls apart, that God is most clearly able to be discerned, waiting only to be invited in. When that choice is made the space which was previously occupied by all that is opposed to God is now wholly available to God, and suffering becomes redemptive, contributing to the ultimate fulfilment of God's purpose to express himself, and live and dance his life in us.

The suffering of Jesus cannot be understood wholly in this way. Far from being the consequence of his own wrong choices it resulted from the abuse of freedom at the hands of others. Jesus had lived totally in union with his Father's will and purpose, and through him the Spirit of life and love had been released. In his passion this was 'set at nought'. He was rejected completely and utterly in a wholly undeserved way. In his very willingness to be reduced, though, to claim nothing exclusively as his own, he revealed God to be the ultimate reality. Jesus' suffering was bound up with his complete givenness to the Father. In this sense his suffering was the result not of a wrong choice, but of the commitment to love, and it is this that takes us into the very heart of suffering, and of its place within God's purpose.

There are many whose suffering, like that of Jesus himself, appears to be completely undeserved. They are the victims of the irresponsibility of others, or sometimes the victims of what might simply be called misfortune. For all that I can acknowledge how I contributed to my own limited experience of suffering, I can also perceive that it was not entirely of my own making. I, personally, had done nothing to bring the painful effects of the threat of an hereditary illness on to myself. It was the consequence of my being in relationship, bound up with others, which is part of the glory of living. From my own perspective, though, I could see all too clearly that what I endured was as nothing compared with what my aunt and cousins had had to suffer, or with what my sister suffered, who was affected far more deeply by the threat of the disease than I was. My suffering, such as it was, was intimately connected with the suffering of others, and is a sign that our ultimate fulfilment in God is not an individual matter alone: the fullness of life is to be received in relationship with the rest of creation. The appearance of Huntington's Disease in my family can be traced back to a selfish choice and wrong action, a rape in fact, which had nothing to do with the immediate members of my family. The existence of such an illness at all, however, is a different matter, so it would seem. We can accept the painful consequences of our own actions, but there are some things which appear to lie beyond anything that human beings may have caused. There are natural disasters, earthquakes, storms, hurricanes and the like, which cause untold suffering. How can such suffering be redemptive?

This takes us at once into the mystery of God, and of his relationship with and intention for his creation. Love is only consummated in freedom. Love cannot be fulfilled by force. Freedom, therefore, has to be part of creation in one way or another if creation is truly to be the embodiment of a God who is love. If human beings are to be free, then the reality of freedom must exist in some measure in the matter from which human consciousness is allowed to emerge. True freedom allows the possibility of wrong choices. Now it is difficult to say what the precise nature of a 'wrong choice' might be at the level of matter which has not yet been raised to consciousness, but it is possible to see how human freedom and love can only emerge in an environment which is not wholly controlled, and, if not wholly controlled, then free to develop in ways which lead to the true realisation of its nature or not.

So called natural disasters would seem to be the product of such an environment, the price of genuine freedom. An illness such as Huntington's Disease may arise for the same reasons, although it is far from being beyond the possibility that wrong choices made by human beings over a long period of time may have contributed to its emergence. We simply do not know everything.

We have, therefore, arrived at a point where we have to conclude that suffering may well simply be the price of freedom, which is itself in the nature of love. Such an intellectualisation, however, is of little comfort to the person suffering intense pain, indeed many may find themselves arguing that the price of freedom is too high and not worth paying. We wonder how such freedom can be justified.

There is indeed only one adequate answer, and it is that God accepts responsibility for it himself; and this is precisely what the suffering of Jesus reveals. Jesus brought his suffering upon himself not as the result of wrong choices or actions but as the direct consequence of love and freedom. In his acceptance of it he revealed the most authentic exercise of freedom ever. He could easily have walked away from the experience, but in Gethsemane he chose to accept what lay before him, freely entrusting himself to the Father. In consenting to be stripped of everything he allowed God to be all, accepting and receiving into himself the total, accumulated effect of freedom, and in so doing he revealed the ultimate nature of love. The freedom to suffer in love is shown to be the very being of God himself. The price of freedom is paid ultimately by God, and in the suffering of Jesus the consummation of love takes place in the meeting of human and divine freedom.

What this means is that in the last resort there is nothing which lies beyond the fulfilment of God's purposes, for all things are in God, and God is in all things. Creation came into being when God breathed his Word, and creation is breathed back to God in the Word incarnate, crucified, raised and glorified. In Christ all things are created, and in him all things are raised to be fulfilled in the love and life of God. The Risen Christ, however, bears the wounds of suffering in his body, which is a sign that the wounds of suffering borne by the whole of creation are indeed to be taken into God, to contribute to the fulfilment of love. The whole of creation is to be the risen body of Christ, and suffering plays its part in the raising up of everything in Christ.

Seemingly undeserved suffering becomes redemptive when we choose to accept it as the inevitable sign of freedom and love. In so doing we allow ourselves to be drawn more deeply into the mystery of Christ, whom we allow to live within us, and who in and through and with us, takes upon and into himself the suffering of the world, to be transformed into his risen body. We then begin to share in the reality of freedom and love, offering ourselves to be part of the means by which love redeems. Herein lies the essence of compassion and intercession, for in suffering with and praying for others, especially those who as yet are unable to bear the burden of their own suffering, we are offering our freedom in the service of love for the sake of Christ:

'I am now rejoicing in my sufferings for your sake, and in my flesh I am completing what is lacking in Christ's afflictions for the sake of his body, that is, the Church. I became its servant according to God's commission that was given to me for you, to make the Word of God fully known, the mystery that has been hidden throughout the ages and generations but has now been revealed to his saints. To them God chose to make known how great among the Gentiles are the riches of the glory of this mystery, which is Christ in you, the hope of glory.'[7]

CHAPTER NINE

Dying

Then on the cross hanged I was,
Where a spear to my heart did glance:
There issued forth both water and blood,
To call my true love to my dance:
Sing O my love, O my love, my love, my love:
This have I done for my true love.

It is sometimes remarked that those who were old enough to have been aware of the event at the time can remember exactly where they were and what they were doing when they heard that President Kennedy had been shot. I am no exception. I was having a piano lesson at home, when my father walked in looking ashen, and broke the news. Although I was only nine years old at the time I was conscious, nevertheless, that this death would send shock waves around the world.

I can also remember with startlingly clarity how I heard of the first death of which I was aware. It was my paternal grandfather's death. I was a little more than five years old and my mother had collected me from school at the end of a day. My brother was in the pram, and my sister and I walked either side of my mother holding on to the pram. I can remember the exact location we had reached when I asked my mother a question, which in the circumstances was extraordinary: I wanted to know where my father was. The extraordinariness of the question lay in the fact that there was no reason why my father should have been with us; he was, after all, at work. Not on this occasion, though. I knew, without being told, that he was not where I should normally have expected him to be. Perhaps I sensed something from my mother, or there was some psychic communication with my father or my grandfather. In answer to my question my mother informed me that my grandfather had just died, and so my father had gone to be with my grandmother. For whatever reason this was so significant an event that from the age of five I could always remember the date, and exactly how I heard of my grandfather's death.

It cannot have been due only to the fact of his death, there must have been other contributory factors, but I grew up with a profound fear of death. Some of it may have had to do with the associated fear of Huntington's Disease, but I was also aware that my grandmother found her husband's death difficult. Whenever we visited her she always cried, and pleaded with us not to leave. At this young age I was acutely aware that death left a painful mark on those who remained and that it was something to be avoided at all possible costs. I had irrational fears, for example, that my grandfather's coffin was still in my grandmother's house. At the first funeral which I attended at the age of eleven I had no idea what to expect. I had never seen a coffin before, I wondered what was to be done with it, and I imagined that the body might even emerge from it. Death was quite literally boxed up, hidden from view, and it was given reality only by the unconscious fears of my imagination.

Not until I was a theological student was I able to confront these anxieties. A multi-disciplinary course at St Christopher's Hospice in London offered the opportunity of examining approaches to death and dying, and I grasped it. At the time I was only dimly aware that this was something I needed to do, and it turned out to be one of the most creative experiences of my life. It was not without discomfort, though. As far as I was concerned I was walking into completely uncharted territory, but I was aware, too, that if I was to minister as a priest, I had to confront my own fears if I was to be of any help at all to others.

The first hurdle was walking past the mortuary as we were being shown around the hospice. I could feel the fear rising within me, in fact the only words that describe adequately how I felt are those associated with death itself: I froze, I was mortified. Fortunately, so I thought at the time, we did not actually go inside. I felt so ashamed of my anxiety, and I was glad that I did not have to reveal it there and then, but I knew that this was a problem which had to be faced sooner or later.

Much of the course was spent as a nursing auxiliary on the wards. As the time approached for me to begin I knew that I had to share my anxiety, which I did with the course tutor, who was nothing but sympathetic and under-standing, and she advised me to do whatever I could, to face whatever I felt able to, but not to push myself into situations with which I felt uncomfortable.

The crisis point was reached about midway through the course. I was assisting a woman suffering with Motor Neurone Disease. Her powers of speech were so dimin-ished that I could scarcely make out what she was saying at all. Clearly she was distressed, and I found it impossible to cope with. It seemed to me that her symptoms were not dissimilar from those of Huntington's Disease and in front of me was a living reminder of all that I feared most. I could stay with her no longer. I went to the Sister's office and broke down.

The staff were wonderful. They assured me that I had no reason to be ashamed, and they listened gently and patiently as I told them something of my family history, of my pain and of my fear. Being able to acknowledge what I felt honestly was the first step towards healing.

The second step came on the last occasion when I went on to the ward as an auxiliary. The nurses knew what I had confronted within. They were aware also that I had not yet faced up to what I still feared: the sight of death itself. Two nurses came to me, told me that a gentleman had just died, that they were performing the last offices for him, and asked if I would like to help. I knew that I had to respond to the invitation. With trepidation I approached the room. Again there were quite irrational fears about what to expect. What I saw, however, was the body of a man looking so peaceful and calm. I stood and looked for a while. The sight of the two nurses so devoid of anxiety was a great help, and I realised that if my deepest fears were to be healed I had to respond to their invitation to assist with the washing of the body. My anxiety level rose again. I swallowed my pride, and like a child asked one of the nurses to hold my hand while I touched the body. For that nurse's sympathetic acceptance of my fear I shall always be grateful.

All went well until the decision was made to turn the body over. As we did so the sound of breath was heard from the body itself. My worst fears seemed to be confirmed! I jumped with fright, almost beside myself with terror! The nurses explained to me that it was not at all uncommon for air to be trapped in the lungs after death, and the movement of the body allowed it to escape. As I left the ward that afternoon I knew that healing had begun to take place.

It is strange to think that such obvious weakness can be turned to strength, but that indeed is how it was, for when I was first ordained I found myself being invited to take up the chaplaincy of a newly-built hospice. Having faced some of my own fears I was asked to be with others as they faced theirs at the point of death itself. One death stands out in my experience above all others, not as it happens from the period of hospice chaplaincy, but from later on. It is the death of Oliver, known as Ollie.

I first met him when he was seventeen years old. Two years prior to that it had been confirmed that he had cancer of the lymph glands. The effect of the illness was vicious. Not only had his education been interrupted, preventing him from taking important exams at the age of sixteen; the illness ravaged his body. Chemotherapy was unsuccessful, and inevitably there was the loss of hair during its course. It gradually dawned upon his parents, his brother, and Ollie himself, that he was going to die.

Understandably there was anger and hostility. Adolescence produces difficulties at the best of times, but to cope with a terminal illness on top of those was hard, to say the least. Ollie wrestled with difficulties, questions and uncertainties: Why? Where was God? Was there a God? Was there life after death? How would he cope with pain?

As his illness progressed he had to cope with increasing bouts of nausea, breathlessness and pain. He tired easily, and he suffered severe depression. His mother, a woman of considerable faith, was a great strength to him, and above all wanted him to grow. Although Ollie would have claimed to be little more than agnostic intellectually in matters of faith, the Prayer of St. Francis became important for him, as well as for his mother. His father found the illness most difficult of all. He was a deeply sensitive man who had survived the concentration camps of Nazi Germany, where his parents had been exterminated. Suffering and pain was written all over his face, and now in the face of his beloved son, he felt the pain of his whole life, and the futility and absurdity of it all.

Whenever I visited Ollie he was always charming and hospitable. He would delight in making me a drink, and his manner was always gentle and courteous. Often it was obvious that he was extremely angry, but he never projected the anger on to me. His parents sometimes bore the brunt of it, and some was directed into his journal, which was allowed to be seen by no one except Ollie himself.

We would talk about all kinds of things, usually about how he felt. We discussed religion, his interests, his hopes and fears. Often there were periods of doubt and even despair. Fluid begin to build up in his lungs and he was forced to pay regular visits to the hospital to have the fluid drained off. Breathlessness became a problem, and his mobility began to be severely restricted.

Ollie struggled and fought for much longer than any of us thought he would. It was a battle against fear as much as anything else, a fear that could be seen in his eyes. The time came when it looked as though the end was very close. He was admitted to hospital, and not realising just how close the end was to be I called on him in hospital unexpectedly. I found Ollie in a state of great distress, finding it very difficult to breathe, and he was dreadfully frightened.

His father could hardly bear it, and longed for something to be done. The doctor tried to reassure and console him, and suggested to Ollie that he could be given an injection to ease his breathlessness, but that this itself would edge him nearer to unconsciousness. Ollie thought for what seemed like hours. Eventually he asked:

'Will it be tonight then?'

'It's very close', the doctor replied.

From that moment the most astonishing sequence of events took place. Ollie took complete control of the situation. Beginning with me, he beckoned me towards him, embraced and kissed me, and said:

'Chris, I love you.'

Then, much more intimately, and as if given a strength hitherto unknown to him, he expressed his love for his parents, thanked them, and told them that he was on the way to something much better. He made his mother promise to pass on to those he knew what he wanted them to know:

'Tell them that I love them all. I love them.'

He asked to make a journey to the toilet, but such was the effort required that almost certainly the pressure on his heart was too great, and without having the injection he lay down on his bed. His breathing had eased of its own accord, and within minutes he had died. So peaceful was his death, that it was not immediately apparent that he had actually breathed his last.

Ollie's death was in marked contrast to much of his life, which cannot be said to have been easy. As he asked the question, 'Will it be tonight, then?' it was with extraordinary courage that he looked death in the face, and in surrendering to its inevitability something new emerged. It was as if the whole of his life was focused in that moment, awaiting a response. In embracing the mystery of death, Ollie was enabled to embrace the mystery of love, and in so doing discover the mystery of life, too. As he accepted the fact of death so his true self revealed itself. Before my very eyes the Father breathed his Spirit of life into Ollie, and in Ollie's broken body Christ was brought to birth within him, and in him Ollie was raised to life. The day of his death was the first of November, the Feast of All Saints. Ollie had not consciously embraced the christian faith, but the mystery of Christ was revealed within him as a gloriously radiant presence, which he will undoubtedly have recognised as the life of God himself in the Communion of Saints.

It is probably true to say that most of us spend most of the time ignoring the reality of death. Coming to terms with it is always something to be done in the future. It is only when the fact of death impinges upon us through the loss of a friend, relative or contemporary that we are brought up short, musing on the fact that it might have been us. Often we are grateful that it was not, and temporary reflections on what is important to and essential about life give way to less weighty matters, until the next time that death reminds us rudely that it waits for us all.

Death appears to be unnatural. It is seen as something which interrupts the flow of life, even renders it meaningless. In essence, though, its purpose is positive, for it offers us the possibility of looking beyond ourselves, away from a world of limitation, to the infinite and eternal God in which all is grounded. This is partly why we find it so difficult to deal with, because it strikes at the heart of our self-centredness and selfishness. Deep within ourselves we know that we are made for relationship and communion, but death, in the sense of the loss of self, the emptiness of self, the giving away of self in love, is necessary for such things to be realised. Our final death is but a symbol of that which is true of the nature of life: that we have to let go in order to receive. Accepting our own mortality is the clue to receiving life in all its fullness.

Such a loss of self seems to ask too much of us, for all we perceive is the loss, and not the fulfilment beyond it. To look beyond, and to give, requires trust and faith. If we are not prepared to face the fact of our mortality we tend to live an illusion of earthly immortality, believing that death can somehow be avoided. It is this, however, which is the real death, for the illusion of immortality in this world builds the self up in its own false strength, separating itself from its only true life in God.

This is the significance of the references to death in the story of the Fall. It is the attempt to secure immortality which results in death:

'Now the serpent was more crafty than any other wild animal that the Lord God had made. He said to the woman, "Did God say, 'You shall not eat from any tree in the garden'?" The woman said to the serpent, "We may eat of the fruit of the trees in the garden: but God said, 'You shall not eat of the fruit of the tree that is in the middle of the garden, nor shall you touch it, or you shall die'." But the serpent said to the woman, "you will not die; for God knows that when you eat of it your eyes will be opened, and you will be like God, knowing good and evil".'[1]

The inner meaning of this story is that when human beings live without reference to God, they themselves take his place, and they believe themselves to be godlike. The attempt to be God without God is indeed an illusion, which death itself ruptures, for it is a reminder that when we can conceive of no reality greater than ourselves we are deeply separated from God and from the truth of our own being. Death in this sense is far more than death to the physical body: it is spiritual death.

This is the death against which St Paul fights:

'For since death came through a human being, the resurrection of the dead has also come through a human being; for as all die in Adam, so all will be made alive in Christ ... The last enemy to be destroyed is death.'[2]

Physical death is a powerful reminder, if ever we needed one, that we are not ourselves the source of life, that the life which we live is indeed a gift from God. When we cling to it, or claim it as a right, it becomes distorted. In the face of death we are completely helpless and powerless. It is precisely this fact, however, which invites us to look beyond ourselves, to the greater reality of God, and return to him, as a response of love, that which he has given in love. Our physical death offers the opportunity for the total consummation of love.

It is true that this takes us beyond a point which we can conceive, but we know it to be true of life as a whole, that growth takes us to a stage beyond where we were before, and that it does so by loss and death. When we are born we simultaneously die to the security of the womb, and only in so doing can we receive life as an individual being. As tiny children we are constantly dying to what we know in order to enter into what is as yet unknown, but the little deaths are of little consequence because the greater reality is natural and exciting. Growth in every sphere of life, and at every level of reality, is always preceded by death, it is indeed the condition of life.

Supremely is it the mark of love, for love can only be known fully if the self is given away to the one who loves in return. When we cling to ourselves we are closed in upon ourselves, and separated in our own isolation. In such circumstances no relationship is possible, and ultimately we die. The willingness to let go of self, however risky it may feel, is the way in which we discover and receive the love which desires to give itself to us; and in the relationship there is far more than the mere sum of two selves: there is a reality infinitely transcending it.

By his death on the cross Jesus demonstrated that our physical death is none other than the ultimate opportunity to give ourselves in love. It cannot have been an easy death. When people die there are often two overwhelming fears: first that they will die in pain, secondly, that they will die alone. In most cases today there is a strong likelihood that fears need not be grounded: pain can be controlled and usually someone can be present with a dying person, unless death comes suddenly and unexpectedly. Of these two fears only one was allayed for Jesus. As well as a whole host of people who taunted him, there was also a handful of friends, and according to St John's Gospel, his mother and the Beloved Disciple, too, who stood and waited with him. It is an obvious fact that only we can die our own death, and in this sense it is a lonely experience, but the presence of those whom we love greatly assists us in the process of letting go, because we are supported by love itself.

It can only be assumed that the pain endured by Jesus was intense. His cry of forsakenness was certainly understood to be a cry of pain, and the offering of vinegar on a sponge was undoubtedly given as an analgesic, but it cannot be thought for one moment, that, even if he drank it, the pain subsided. To give oneself in love in such circumstances is truly remarkable.

Yet, what we glean from the gospels is that Jesus' attention was not in the slightest self-focused. In their varying ways the evangelists show that Jesus was concerned for others and for his Father. According to St Luke Jesus' concerns were for the forgiveness of those who did to him that of whose real import they were unaware:

'Father, forgive them, for they do not know what they are doing.'[3]

According to St John Jesus set his affairs in order by ensuring that his mother was looked after:

'When Jesus saw his mother and the disciple whom he loved standing beside her, he said to his mother, "Woman, here is your son." Then he said to the disciple, "Here is your mother." And from that hour the disciple took her into his own home.'[4]

St Matthew and St Mark alike characterise Jesus' spiritual pain in the cry of forsakenness from the cross, quoting words from Psalm 22:

'My God, my God, why have you forsaken me?'[5]

Even this experience of abandonment was accepted as the consequence of his self-giving in love to the Father, the ultimate sign of love, when love itself seems not to be reciprocated.

Jesus died as he had lived: in a spirit of utter selflessness, and in so dying he could only trust that his Father would not ultimately abandon him. He could not have known for sure, though, and in that sense he was less fortunate than we are, for on the strength of his resurrection, we are able to entrust ourselves to the Father in death, knowing that if we do just that, we do not face oblivion, but the fulfilment and consummation of love.

Death is the one unavoidable fact of life. By learning to die daily death is transformed from something to be feared into the opportunity for giving in love. To my mind it is not at all insignificant or coincidental that when Ollie decided that the death which had been staring him in the face for so long was no longer to be avoided, but embraced, then love and life were released deep within him. For life and death, and death and resurrection, are but part of the same unifying reality of love, which we can know before, in and beyond our physical death.

CHAPTER TEN

Rising

Then down to hell I took my way
For my true love's deliverance,
And rose again on the third day,
Up to my true love and the dance:
Sing O my love, O my love, my love, my love;
This have I done for my true love.

There is a moment at sunrise and sunset when night turns to day, and day turns to night. The moment is identical in each. There is a space, a still point, when the instant which follows the setting of the sun might just as well be that which precedes its rising.

In between the exhalation and inhalation of breath is another point of stillness, when the yielding of the spirit in death might equally as well be the pause before life is breathed in again.

In the same way there is a point where tears and laughter are indistinguishable from each other, and it is perfectly possible to misinterpret one for the other.

The miracle of resurrection occurs in this twilight dimension of reality, as night is on the verge of turning to day, as the body awaits the inhalation of breath, and as tears of sorrow give way to the joy of laughter.

It is sometimes commented that the resurrection narratives in the gospels are unreliable, that they are inconsistent with each other, and that it is impossible to know what really happened. Far from being something to lament this is actually cause for rejoicing, for the inability to pin the resurrection down is the clearest possible sign of its authenticity. To say that it is a mystery is not to give in to intellectual sloppiness or laziness: it is to acknowledge that the resurrection transcends all boundaries of thought and expectation. It is the breaking through of a dimension of reality which is beyond our ordinary senses and rational capacities. Once we are open to the reality of resurrection, though, we are renewed at every level of our being, we are raised to new awareness and to newness of life.

The gospels seek to communicate an experience, which is infinitely beyond our minds to comprehend in terms of what is known before resurrection. They mediate an intuitive awareness of God, as do the creation stories in Genesis, which can only be received if preceded by a death, a surrender of our whole being. When that is done, however, we enter into an awareness which infinitely transcends all previous experience, and yet which embraces that experience and raises it to the new dimension of reality. In that awareness there is a direct, intuitive knowledge of the Risen Christ in the depths of our being.

This is not, however, a self-induced experience. Anyone who has truly experienced the reality of resurrection could never possibly suggest that, for it is precisely our inability to do anything in our own strength, which allows the miracle of resurrection to take place. From beyond us the Father breathes his Spirit of life into us again and raises us to life in Christ.

The resurrection of Christ is sheer mystery, a mystery which transforms the whole of creation. It is a glorious and liberating mystery, which sets us progressively free from limitation with life and love. The resurrection life is our natural habitat, into which the whole creative process is being drawn in Christ.

The gospels struggle with the attempt to contain what cannot be contained, to describe what cannot be described. They bear witness to the miracle of resurrection which hovers between disbelief and belief, doubt and faith, death and life. There is no adequate conceptual framework to explain or characterise it. It can only be pointed to in an elusive and mysterious way.

In all of the accounts there is a strong element of ambiguity. Together what they do is to mediate the experience of resurrection as a transition from one state of awareness and being into another. This ambiguity is represented immediately by the fact that the timing of the visit to the tomb is said to vary. St Mark's Gospel suggests that the visit follows sunrise:

'When the Sabbath was over, Mary Magdalene, and Mary the mother of James, and Salome bought spices, so that they might go and anoint him. And very early on the first day of the week, when the sun had risen, they went to the tomb.'[1]

This is in marked contrast to St John's Gospel where the visit precedes sunrise:

'Early on the first day of the week, while it was still dark, Mary Magdalene came to the tomb and saw that the stone had been removed from the tomb.'[2]

For St. Matthew the visit occurs just as the sun is rising:

'After the Sabbath, as the first day of the week was dawning, Mary Magdalene and the other Mary went to see the tomb.'[3]

The same is true of St Luke:

'But on the first day of the week, at early dawn, they came to the tomb, taking the spices that they had prepared.'[4]

For some these discrepancies are a real cause of difficulty: they cannot all be 'true', so it is argued. It might well be suggested that the passage of time between sunrise and just after is minimal, but this would be to approach the matter at the wrong level, and in the wrong spirit, and thus to miss the point, which is that the very experience itself is mysterious, elusive and ambiguous. Only by sign and symbol can it be conveyed. Such elusiveness is present in all of the narratives, and it is this very quality which testifies to its authenticity. For the knowledge of resurrection is indeed one that gradually 'dawns' in our awareness.

St Mark's Gospel contains the most stark of all the accounts. The rolling away of the stone is the evidence that the resurrection is not the result of human initiative, indeed it is beyond our capacity to know how it happens, for it is the miracle of life itself, whose source is God alone. Similarly the words of the young man dressed in white concerning the whereabouts of Jesus indicate that the knowledge and experience of resurrection is one that comes from beyond:

'But he said to them, "Do not be alarmed: you are looking for Jesus of Nazareth, who was crucified. He has been raised; he is not here. Look, there is the place they laid him. But go, tell his disciples and Peter that he is going ahead of you to Galilee".'[5]

What is being conveyed here is the sense that resurrection is new, unpredictable, unimaginable, almost inconceivable. The visitors to the tomb were bound, as it were, quite understandably, but bound nevertheless to a dimension of reality which had now been transcended, and from which they were to be raised, too. The sheer incomprehensibility of this glorious truth is communicated by the fact that they were afraid:

'So they went out and fled from the tomb, for terror and amazement had seized them; and they said nothing to anyone, for they were afraid.'[6]

It might be some cause for surprise that the reaction to such good news should be fear, but we know only too well from our own experience that we can react to opposites in the same way. Bad news and good news alike can be greeted with disbelief if they are unexpected. So, too, the liberation that comes with resurrection can be met with fear initially, precisely because it leads us into a new dimension of reality and experience, and when we enter into the genuinely unknown there is both apprehension and excitement which comes with the loss of control.

St Matthew's Gospel follows St Mark's account closely, but there are one or two differences which are significant. First of all the news of resurrection is received not only with fear:

'So they left the tomb quickly with fear and great joy, and ran to tell his disciples.'[7]

Secondly, Jesus himself is recognised as being present to them:

'Suddenly Jesus met them and said, "Greetings!" And they came to him, took hold of his feet, and worshipped him. Then Jesus said to them, "Do not be afraid; go and tell my brothers to go to Galilee; there they will see me".'[8]

The addition of these two features, compared with St Mark's version, points to something far more subtle than, and in a totally different dimension from, mere inconsistency. Rather they show how the knowledge of the truth and reality of resurrection dawns. Fear and disbelief do indeed turn to joy in all kinds of circumstances, as we gradually realise that we have been presented with something incomprehensible, yet wonderful. At first we register only incredulity and shock, but as we grasp the full import of what has happened, so joy emerges. This was precisely the experience of those who came to know the reality of resurrection first, and it is this that the narrative seeks to mediate.

Secondly, however, what gradually dawned upon them was that the life that was being released in them, and was raising them to a new level of awareness, was none other than the life that was released in them through Jesus before his death, although experienced in a new way. Indeed it could only be accounted for by the realisation that it was the life of Jesus himself being released from beyond death. The source of their life was Jesus raised from the dead.

That this realisation should have been gradual is not surprising either. It is common knowledge that if we look directly into the sun or into another bright light our eyes are temporarily blinded as a result. We simply cannot cope with the strength of the light, and it takes time for our eyes to adjust. Mystical awareness is quite familiar with this as an analogy for a direct, intuitive experience of God. The knowledge of God in the depths of our being deprives us of our customary ways of knowing and seeing, and we then proceed to know by unknowing, to see by not seeing. Then the darkness itself gradually becomes a luminous darkness.

The experience of resurrection is indeed mystical, as St Paul's experience of the Risen Christ on the Damascus Road illustrates all too well. It is quite beyond our 'normal' level of experience, and yet at the same time it is as natural to us as the air we breathe. What occurs is a change of consciousness, of awareness. This is precisely what happened to those who came to know the resurrection first, and what happens ultimately to all who come to know it after them. The initial revelation was blinding, hence the occurrence of disbelief and disorientation. Gradually, however, as the truth dawned, so, too, did a new way of seeing and knowing, and to that awareness the presence of Jesus, raised from the dead, was revealed. The form of his presence, however, was not as it had been before, because Jesus himself had entered into a new dimension of reality. The form was mysterious and beyond comprehension, a spiritual body, and as soon as it had been thought to be grasped it disappeared from sight.

This is the experience conveyed in the wonderful story of the two disciples on the road to Emmaus in St Luke's Gospel. At first they are not aware of the presence of the Risen Lord with them:

'While they were talking and discussing, Jesus himself came near and went with them, but their eyes were kept from recognising him.'[9]

Gradually their awareness is raised to the point where they recognise him, but in that moment he disappears:

'When he was at the table with them, he took bread,

blessed and broke it, and gave it to them. Then their eyes were opened, and they recognised him; and he vanished from their sight. They said to each other, "Were not our hearts burning within us while he was talking to us on the road, while he was opening the scriptures to us?" '[10]

Here the awareness has progressed to an inward one, in which the Risen Christ is truly known to be dwelling in the depths of their being. This is the significance of the question, 'Were not our hearts burning within us?' Does this mean that the awareness and knowledge of resurrection is a purely subjective one? Here the words 'subjective' and 'objective' are unsatisfactory and inadequate, for the knowledge of God is not objective, if, by which, is meant that he is known as one object among many. He is the reality in which all things are grounded, and the true knowledge of anything is revealed only in relation to him. We can only know God as we are in relationship with him, but in that relationship the duality of subject and object is transcended in love. This is the ultimate experience of God which is symbolised by the doctrine of the trinity, which affirms that God is a relationship of love, in which distinction is embraced in communion. Such knowledge is beyond our ordinary rational consciousness, indeed it can never be known objectively, as something outside ourselves; it can only be known inwardly and subjectively, in fact, by love alone.

In this sense the resurrection can only be known subjectively, too, not as something external to ourselves, but as the life of the Eternal Word, in and through whom we come to be, and by whose incarnation, death, resurrection and ascension we are raised to the fullness of life in God, to participate without reserve in the mutual exchange of love between Father and Son in the Spirit. The resurrection can only be known subjectively, but when it is so known it is known to be not just an individual reality, but the very life of the universe, breaking out in history, and transforming all things in Christ.

The reality of resurrection is to be perceived outwardly in lives that are changed and transfigured. In this sense the outward manifestation of resurrection lies in the birth of the Church itself. Not by any stretch of the imagination could those first disciples have simply persuaded themselves that with the death of Jesus nothing significant had changed. Anyone who has been bereaved knows how ludicrous it is to be told to 'cheer up', or to 'pull yourself out of it'. In such circumstances life has disappeared, and no amount of persuasion will convince that nothing very much has changed. The first disciples were utterly demoralised by the death of Jesus. In him they had lost just about everything. Yet within less than three days, far less than a period needed for bereavement to work its course, they were transformed into people of life and joy, willing to explain the transformation as the inexplicable, to describe it as the indescribable. However slowly the fullness of truth dawned they knew that there was only one explanation for it: that the Risen Christ was present within and among them. The place of transformation for all who experience the reality of resurrection is precisely the place where life has been inhibited and blocked, and this is exactly what St John's Gospel portrays in relation to Mary Magdalene, Thomas and Peter.

Mary Magdalene is depicted as one searching for the deceased. This is not at all an uncommon experience of those who are newly bereaved. The loss cannot be accepted easily. Gradually the process of grieving leads to an acceptance of the loss, and in that moment, life is received anew and the bereaved person begins to live with a new strength and purpose. Some people find it very difficult to be brought to this point. The old memories and former ways are clung to in possessive ways that keep the bereaved stuck at the stage where death occurred. It is not uncommon, for example, for the room of the deceased to be kept exactly as it was when he or she was alive. It reveals an inability to accept the fact of loss, and this is a resistance to growth and life.

It would seem that Mary Magdalene displayed a tendency to cling to the past, to the familiar, to the known. In this respect she reveals to us an aspect of ourselves, for we all resist the flow of life within us to a greater or lesser degree. When she discovered Jesus' body to be missing, she alone stayed at the tomb:

'But Mary stood weeping outside the tomb. As she wept, she bent over to look into the tomb; and she saw two angels in white, sitting where the body of Jesus had been lying, one at the head and the other at the feet. They said to her, "Woman, why are you weeping?" She said to them, "They have taken away my Lord, and I do not know where they have laid him." When she had said this she turned around and saw Jesus standing there, but she did not know that it was Jesus.'[11]

Tears, of course, are the natural expression of grief, but with time grief gives way, and life is resumed in a new way, when the old relationship has been allowed to die. Mary Magdalene is depicted as looking for a continuation of the old life. Her inability to recognise Jesus standing before her is entirely typical: we rarely recognise the new form of life offered to us at first. As recognition occurred, however, her reaction was instinctive:

'Jesus said to her "Mary!" She turned and said to him "Rabbouni!" (which means Teacher). Jesus said to her, "Do not hold on to me, because I have not yet ascended to the Father. But go to my brothers and say to them, 'I am ascending to my Father and your Father, to my God and your God'." Mary Magdalene went and announced to the disciples, "I have seen the Lord"; and she told them that he had said these things to her.'[12]

Mary Magdalene was met by the Resurrection at the very place where she resisted life: her possessiveness, her tendency to cling. Her immediate reaction when she realised who stood before her was to hold on to him. It was here that she needed to be free, for only by learning to let go could she enter into the fullness of life. The reality of the resurrection was made known to her exactly where life was blocked, and this was her point of transformation.

Thomas is someone who has a very contemporary feel about him: he is doubtful and sceptical. This was his weakness, however, the place where he resisted growth and life. Not being prepared to trust the experience of others he insisted that he would not accept the claim that the Lord had been raised, and seen by the others, unless he had evidence. He represents the all too common stance that reality is restricted to that which can be known to the senses and to reason alone. This kind of person finds it difficult, almost impossible, to surrender to a reality greater than themselves, and states all kinds of conditions which are to be fulfilled, before their position is to be changed. The burden of proof is laid at the feet of those who represent an alternative view.

The significance of Thomas' acceptance of the reality of resurrection lies in the fact that it was not the other disciples who convinced him, for he was blind to the transformation that had self-evidently been effected in them, but the Risen Lord himself. He was met at his point of weakness and taken beyond it, indeed reprimanded for the inadequacy of his position:'Then he said to Thomas, "Put your finger here and see my hands. Reach out your hand and put it in my side. Do not doubt but believe." Thomas answered him, "My Lord and my God!" Jesus said to him, "Have you believed because you have seen me? Blessed are those who have not seen and yet have come to believe." '[13]

The challenge to Thomas was to trust, to believe that reality is far more mysterious than he would allow, and to acknowledge that what is to be known could not be confined and restricted to what he alone perceived. In him is represented the truth that the knowledge available to the sense and reason has its part to play, indeed is essential, in leading us to the awareness of the mystery of God, but that it has limits and that if the fullness of that knowledge is to be received it has to be transcended.

The transformation of Peter is in many ways the most touching of all. Of all the disciples he seems to have been the most impulsive and headstrong: he would commit all or nothing of himself. Furthermore it would seem that he would do so before thinking it through. His protestations to Jesus before the crucifixion, that he would never let him down, must have returned to haunt him in the light of his denial. Inwardly he must have accused himself of failure, as we do with ourselves time and time again. Failure leads to a loss of confidence, a loss of esteem, and a sense of shame.

The knowledge of the resurrection must have come to Peter, at first, as something of a mixed blessing. Almost certainly his initial reaction would have been one of delight, but this must have been accompanied with a more intense awareness of his own weakness. Might it not have been the case that he expected a reprimand such as Thomas received?

The truth of the matter is that Peter was transformed by the Risen Lord's confidence in him. From a position of failing himself he was raised to new heights in the leading of others. This is what lies behind the charge to feed the lambs and tend the sheep.[14] Peter's weakness was to commit himself to more than he was capable of on his own, but, strengthened by the Risen Christ within, he was able, ultimately, to fulfil his commitment to die a martyr's death.

The characterisations of Mary Magdalene, Thomas and Peter in St John's Gospel show that the evidence of the resurrection is to be seen in its capacity to effect transformation at the point of resistance to life, and death. The sign of this transforming life is the Church itself, whose very existence bears witness to the presence of the Risen Christ. After Jesus was condemned to death the body of his disciples was also broken apart as they fled from the scene. Jesus had brought them together and with his death came their disintegration and separation. The resurrection was known in its power to draw together that which had been separated and broken, both in respect of Jesus' own body and soul, and also in respect of the broken community of his followers, and bring about integration and unity. This is not to suggest that the Church is perfect; only that the resurrection is its charter, and its purpose is to bear witness to that which is happening all the time at the heart of reality, for the Resurrection is cosmic in its ultimate nature. The calling of the Church is to embody in itself the mystery of Christ, enlivened by the Spirit, released in all its fullness at Pentecost. It is to be a sign that it participates in a reality which is infinitely beyond it, yet which is revealed in its own life. This sign is not for itself alone, though. It is to point to the truth that the whole of creation is grounded in God, and that by means of the Spirit at work in all things and in all people it is to be raised and transformed in Christ to be brought into complete union with the Father.

The empty tomb is a sign that matter, represented in the physical body of Jesus, is ultimately to be transformed into the spiritual body of Christ, in and through whom all things exist, and by whose resurrection are raised. The resurrection, therefore, penetrates the lowest form of life, and little by little it is transformed by the Spirit into the Body of Christ. No part of Creation is to be left out of this glorious process. Indeed the whole of creation is imbued with the life and presence of the Spirit, who is ceaselessly at work transforming and raising everything into the fullness of life in Christ.

We begin to glimpse something of this profound and mysterious truth in our own lives when we have been touched by the reality of the Risen Christ, for all the dimensions of body, mind and spirit are gradually raised into a greater harmony and union, both within themselves, and with the rest of creation. We become more deeply aware that we are far from being separated from material reality, indeed we are very much part of it, but that all reality, because it is indwelt by the Spirit is gradually being transformed into the fullness of Christ, to contribute to the offering of love made in, by and through him to the Father. Every dimension of reality, physical, psychical and spiritual, is to be raised and fulfilled to participate in the mystery of Christ.

Every occasion, when the resistance to life surrenders to the onward flow of life, is a participation in and a sign of the presence of the Risen Christ. We know the reality of the resurrection wherever and whenever death, in whatever form, is transcended and transformed into life. Here the original purpose of God, deflected by sin, that creation should come into being in the Eternal Word, expressive of God's own being, and enlivened by God's Spirit, is restored and fulfilled in Christ. When we awaken to the reality of resurrection we begin to see that all things already participate in it, and are being drawn towards their completion in Christ, which is the very purpose of existence:

'He is the image of the invisible God, the firstborn of all creation; for in him all things in heaven and on earth were created, things visible and invisible, whether thrones or dominions or rulers or powers – all things have been created through him and for him. He himself is before all things and in him all things hold together. He is the head of the body, the Church; he is the beginning, the first-born from the dead, so that he might come to have first place in everything.'[15]

CHAPTER ELEVEN

Realising

Then up to heaven I did ascend,
Where now I dwell in sure substance
On the right hand of God, that man
May come unto the general dance:
Sing O my love, O my love, my love, my love;
This have I done for my true love.

In the closing chapters of the final book in the Bible, the mysterious and enigmatic Revelation to John, the fulfilment of all things is characterised in terms of a marriage:

'Then I saw a new heaven and a new earth: for the first earth had passed away, and the sea was no more. And I saw the holy city, the new Jerusalem, coming down out of heaven from God, prepared as a bride adorned for her husband. And I heard a loud voice from the throne saying,

"See, the home of God is
among mortals.
He will dwell with them
they will be his peoples,
and God himself will be with
them;
he will wipe away every tear
from their eyes.
Death will be no more;
mourning and crying and pain
will be no more,
for the first things have passed
away."

And the one who was seated on the throne said,

"See, I am making all things new".'[1]

The vision continues to describe the bride:
'Then one of the seven angels who had the seven bowls full of the seven last plagues came and said to me,
"Come, I will show you the bride, the wife of the lamb."
And in the spirit he carried me away to a great, high mountain and showed me the holy city Jerusalem coming down out of heaven from God. It has the glory of God and a radiance like a very rare jewel, like jasper, clear as crystal ...
I saw no temple in the city, for its temple is the Lord God the Almighty and the lamb. And the city has no need of sun or moon to shine on it, for the glory of God is its light, and its lamp is the lamb. The nations will walk by its light, and the kings of the earth will bring their glory into it.'[2]

The consummation of all things can only be alluded to in images and symbols, for the knowledge and awareness of God completely transcends, and thereby transforms us. The symbol of marriage is an evocative one, for the end of our journey towards the fullness of life is the realisation of God in us, and us in him, a complete union in love. John characterises this union as one in which we, the bride, the holy city, are completely transparent to God, reflecting his glory, whose very being is the source of our light and life. Here, by means of image and symbol, the mystical vision alludes to the fulfilment of love, the realisation of God in us, and us in him. Love gives birth to its own knowledge, almost demanding a new language, and passing eventually into the language of silence alone.

The marriage, the union, is between the earthly and the heavenly, the human and the divine. As a symbol of our union with God marriage is not unusual. In St Matthew's Gospel, for example, Jesus refers to the kingdom of heaven in terms of a marriage:

'Once more Jesus spoke to them in parables, saying:

"The kingdom of heaven may be compared to a king who gave a wedding banquet for his son".'[3]

The wedding banquet is a symbol of the life of the kingdom, in which those who are invited feast with God to celebrate the fulfilment of love.

In the prophecy of Hosea unfaithfulness in a human marriage becomes the means of insight into the faithfulness of God's love, hinting already that human love and divine love have much in common.

The symbol of marriage is represented in a very strong way in the Song of Solomon, too. This exquisite love poetry has been understood variously as celebrating the love between human bride and bridegroom, and also as an allegory of the relationship between God and Israel, and between God and the individual soul. It is in the tradition of the best poetry that we should not feel constrained to choose between any of these interpretations, but rather delight in its ambiguity and suggestiveness, for in its capacity to evoke, lies the possibility of holding seemingly separate and contrasting dimensions of experience and reality in union. That such gloriously sensual imagery can be appreciated as speaking of God is a sign that sexual and mystical union, matter and spirit, earth and heaven, are all ultimately part of the same reality and mystery of divine love.

At its best marriage is the means by which husband and wife allow each to be wholly present to the other. Complete openness at the level of body, mind and spirit brings about a union in which two people are both distinct, and also totally at one. There are no barriers or defences, so that each can give their whole being to the other, and in return receive the other's being. In love husband and wife are fully present to each other at every level of their being.

With the ascension of Jesus is realised the possibility of God and creation being wholly present to each other, completely at one in love. In the ascension of Jesus to the Father all barriers of time and space and limitation are broken down and transcended, so that the whole of created and human experience is taken up into God himself. The marriage of heaven and earth has taken place in the incarnation of Christ; in his life and death God has revealed his presence in the very depths of human experience, and in the resurrection and ascension God has raised up and taken into himself the total experience of creation, so that in Christ God and creation can be wholly present to each other. God is not denied entry into any aspect of creation's life and being, nor is creation barred from the fullness of life in God. Christ himself is the focal point, the one in whom the marriage of the divine and the human takes place, and by means of the Spirit, released anew at Pentecost, all things are being drawn into Christ, to participate to the full in the love shared between Father and Son in the Spirit. In Christ the human and the divine have complete access to each other. As the Risen Christ ascends to the Father, so, paradoxically, he is not taken from us; rather, because the Father is the ground and source of everything, who expresses himself, and brings everything into being, in the Eternal Word, and who is present in everything in the Spirit, and yet infinitely transcends all things, so the Risen Christ transcends all barriers to become fully present in the whole of creation. Precisely because of this the whole of creation is offered the possibility of realising God in itself through Christ. In him we are brought into union with God, so that he can be wholly present to us, and we to him.

The key to the realisation of this presence of God in creation lies simply in being wholly aware and totally given to the present moment. The very image of Christ's ascension teases us, because we tend to think of it in terms of distance away. In truth it is the exact opposite: it is the passing beyond barriers of time and space into the realm of eternity, and in the dimension of eternity there is only the present moment, the here and now! It comes as something of a surprise, therefore, to realise that in essence we are being brought to where we are. It is as simple as that. And as difficult as that, too, for we do not find it easy to be where we are: we are distracted by so many things, and we believe that life is far more complicated than just living in the full awareness of the present moment. Yet, if we are wholly given to the present moment we are also brought to the awareness of the presence of Christ in that moment. This is one of the truths revealed in the story of the meeting of Jesus and the Samaritan woman at Jacob's well in St John's Gospel.[4]

The awareness of Jesus himself contrasts directly with that of the woman with whom he comes into contact. He is presented to us as one who is tired out by a journey, and rests by the well in the heat of the day. In this picture we are given something so simple that it is likely to pass us by. Jesus is completely in touch with himself, aware of his needs, and able to stop and wait. In all the circumstances and pressures of life he knew when and how to relax, and this is a far cry from the awareness and attitude of most of us. The lack of awareness in relation to ourselves, to others and to God, in the stillness of the present moment, leads to the fragmentation and disintegration of our own souls, and the very fabric of our being as it is grounded in God, and as it is in relationship to others. In stillness and the silent awareness of the present moment we allow the possibility of our soul's refreshment and healing.

The conversation opens with a simple request from Jesus of the woman:

' "Give me a drink".'[5]

From here on Jesus seeks to lead the woman into the awareness of her true self by encouraging her to give her complete attention to him in the fullness of the present. It becomes immediately clear, however, how far she is from this. The blissfully simple and straightforward request for a drink is the trigger which reveals the extent of her distraction. The relationship is seen to be coloured by a whole history of racial, religious and cultural antagonism. The woman is not wholly exceptional in this respect, but it is a telling indictment, nevertheless, of our human condition. The request that a basic human need be answered and met is immediately complicated by extraneous matters.

This is indeed the condition in which all of us find ourselves most of the time. We bring to every situation, to every relationship, a history, which in some instances has nothing whatever to do with the matter in hand, in fact it prevents our attention from being focused clearly and unreservedly. Our minds are incessantly active, planning, organising, projecting, engaged in anything other than complete attention to what presents itself to us in the moment, and thereby we fail to see what is there

Little by little Jesus seeks to lead her into a fuller and deeper awareness. He helps her to be in touch with herself, no longer evading her true desires and feelings, but accepting of them, and as a result she is led into the truth about herself. She is nudged from a state of distractedness towards integration, and, therefore, attentiveness to the real nature of the situation and the moment in which she finds herself.

The way in which this awareness is brought to birth is by being attentive to the very practical circumstances of life: the woman has come to the well to draw water. For many of us the mundane necessities of life are perceived to be a distraction from what is thought to be really important. We deceive ourselves by thinking that if only we can be relieved of such hindrances then we would be able to give ourselves to what really matters. Yet the truth is that the mundane necessities of life will always be with us. What makes the difference is our attitude towards them.

The woman, not surprisingly, reacts favourably to the prospect of no longer having to be bothered with the daily drudgery of coming to the well to draw water. When Jesus offers her living water the woman becomes a little more aware of herself, perhaps of her irritation and frustration, which is an indication of her inattentiveness and distraction, and she says:

'"Sir, give me this water, so that I may never be thirsty or have to keep coming here to draw water".'[6]

Now that Jesus has been successful in engaging her attention he is able to lead her into the full awareness of the source of her frustration. More often than not what presents itself as frustration in one aspect of life, usually an apparently superficial one, is actually an outlet for a deeper dissatisfaction elsewhere. The woman's desire for a better life, expressed in the enthusiasm to be relieved from the need to draw water each day, is shown to be the desire for something far more profound, as Jesus indicates when he asks her to call her husband. With this command Jesus penetrates to the heart of her distraction: her desire for love.

It would seem that she has been unsuccessful in her relationships: there have been five husbands, and now another relationship. In this very fact is the suggestion that she has been unable to give herself fully to any one person, and that the point has always been reached when she has been tempted to look elsewhere. This is so true of all of us. Something better, fuller, more satisfying always seems to be over the horizon, anywhere but where we are. Undoubtedly we are invariably hurt and wounded by the actions, attitudes, infidelities and frustrations of others, but we all tend also to avoid looking within ourselves, to see what we contribute to the unsatisfactoriness of our circumstances. Continually looking beyond ourselves, and blaming external sources, is a way of avoiding a full encounter with the truth. Until we are prepared to accept responsibility for ourselves we shall always be restless and dissatisfied.

By this stage of the conversation the woman has come a long way. She is indeed allowing herself to be led into the truth of herself, and in so doing she is becoming less distracted and more focused, more aware of the real nature of what is happening in the moment. Her attention becomes more and more given, in fact, to the person in whose presence she finds herself. Here, too, we can see ourselves so clearly. So often our real attention is far from being given to the person offered to us in the present moment. We may be prevented from giving our attention to the other person by our preoccupation with matters which are quite unrelated to them. Alternatively we may create the other person in an image of our own making, and fail to see them as they really are, rather than as we think they are. The woman actually becomes interested in who it is who is with her. His remarkable psychic insight impresses her, and because of this she realises that he is something different, someone who might be able to fulfil what she is looking for. Her awareness has been taken beyond the need for human relationships and love, to their source and ground. She is being drawn to her desire for God.

In this final stage of the conversation the attention is focused on the way in which the reality of God is known and expressed. Jesus takes her beyond the barriers erected by religion itself. This is something that we ourselves are reluctant to face. The mystery of God infinitely transcends everything, although it reveals itself in everything. In pointing to the reality of God we inevitably limit God by what we say and think. We have to use words, signs and symbols to express the mystery of God, and the exact choice of such things is profoundly important. Yet it still remains the case that when we have expressed the mystery as precisely as we can our expression falls far short of the mystery and the reality. Only by going beyond into the silence of eternity do we truly know what the words, the signs and the symbols are seeking to convey.

In most of our experience we allow ourselves to be distracted at the precise stage when we are on the verge of realising the presence of God. We find ourselves embroiled in endless disputes about how the reality and the mystery of God is to be pointed to, rather than by being attentive to that reality in the silent awareness of the present moment. The consequence is that we fail to realise God in favour of our distracted and fragmented selves.

The woman, having come thus far, enters into religious disputation: who is in possession of the truth? Her ancestors worshipped on the mountain; Jesus stands in the tradition which claims that worship in the temple at Jerusalem is the true worship. Jesus leads her beyond both:

' "Woman, believe me, the hour is coming when you will worship the Father neither on this mountain nor in Jerusalem. You worship what you do not know; we worship what we know, for salvation is from the Jews. But the hour is coming, and is now here, when the true worshippers will worship the Father in spirit and truth, for the Father seeks such as these to worship him. God is spirit, and those who worship him must worship in spirit and truth".'[7]

Jesus claims that the tradition in which he stands is in fact more authentic than hers, but he leads her to the point when it becomes clear that the reality and the mystery to which all religious traditions claim to point, his and hers included, infinitely transcends them, even those which may believe themselves to be more authentic than any others. The reality to which they all point is the mystery of Christ himself, who is beyond all limitation, and yet present always and everywhere.

As she is taken beyond the point of argument so she is delivered from all her distractions, to be able to focus completely on who it is who is present to her. Her attention turns towards the one who is yet to come, and who is expected to reveal the mystery, which is the subject of their conversation:

'The woman said to him, "I know that Messiah is

coming" (who is called Christ)."When he comes, he will proclaim all things to us." '8

With her attention firmly fixed beyond anything which she can already claim to know fully, Jesus is able to focus her attention precisely on where she is:

'Jesus said to her, "I am he, the one who is speaking to you".'9

In the complete attentiveness to the present moment the woman is able to receive the revelation of who it is who is present to her in that moment. It has not been her feelings, her thoughts or her actions which has brought his presence to her. He has been present all along, but she was not aware of it. Only by letting go of her preoccupations, her masks and her defence mechanisms could she be brought to full attentiveness in the present moment, and in that moment become aware of the presence of Christ.

This is indeed the pattern of creation. God is present to us at every moment, although we fail to be aware. The path to that awareness lies in allowing ourselves to be wholly and fully present to whatever matter is to hand. As we do so Christ reveals himself, and God realises his presence in us.

The mystery of this realisation is what the liturgy of the church, and supremely the Eucharist, discloses. In word, sign and symbol the reality of Christ, in whom God and creation are at one, married, wholly present to each other, is revealed. In the comparatively short time that it takes to say the Eucharistic Prayer, the mystery in which everything is grounded, the reality of God himself, is allowed to be made present with devastating simplicity. In this prayer are two partners, God and us, who dance in the one reality of Christ, united in love and attention.

The bread and wine represent the whole of creation. As they are offered and placed on the altar just before the Eucharistic Prayer so this signifies the awareness that creation exists to be the expression of God's love and being in Christ. Only in Christ does it realise what it truly is. Apart from the life-giving action of the Spirit it has no life, the presence of Christ is not realised, and we are separated from the Father, the ground of our being. The placing of the bread and wine on the altar signifies our desire that the mystery of Christ should be realised in us.

The Eucharistic Prayer has three sections. In the first we recognise the way in which God is present to us: to begin with it is acknowledged that he is present in the very act of creation in and through Christ:

> 'For he is your living Word;
> through him you have created all things from the beginning,
> and formed us in your own image.'[10]

He is present, too, in the life, death, resurrection and ascension of Jesus,

> 'Through him you have freed us from the
> slavery of sin,
> giving him to be born as man and to die upon the cross;
> you raised him from the dead
> and exalted him to your right hand on high.'[11]

He is present in the Spirit, the breath of life,

> 'Through him you have sent upon us
> your holy and life-giving Spirit,
> and made us a people for your own possession.'[12]

In the second section is disclosed the mystery of the realisation of Christ in Jesus through the action of the Spirit in the Incarnation. All the time, however, the dynamic of the Eucharistic Prayer reveals that by our incorporation into Christ the mystery of Christ is realised in us, too. The bread and wine, tokens of the whole of creation, ourselves included, become the focus by which the presence of Christ is known. Our ascent to the Father is preceded, however, by the divine descent. Just as the Spirit breathes

the life of God into Creation itself, so the action of the
Spirit in the Incarnation is recalled, and the need to be
indwelt by the Spirit if we are to realise Christ acknowledged:

> 'Accept our praises, heavenly Father,
> through your Son our Saviour Jesus Christ;
> and as we follow his example and obey his command,
> grant that by the power of your Holy Spirit
> these gifts of bread and wine
> may be to us his body and his blood.'[13]

With the words of institution God's descent in the total
offering of Jesus is complete. In the self-giving love
revealed on the cross creation is restored to God. The
divine descent is complemented by the ascent of creation
in Christ to the Father. In the third section of the prayer
this aspect of the dynamic is expressed: our whole being is
offered to the Father in Christ:

> 'Accept through him, our great high priest,
> this our sacrifice of thanks and praise;
> and as we eat and drink these holy gifts
> in the presence of your divine majesty,
> renew us by your Spirit,
> inspire us with your love,
> and unite us in the body of your Son,
> Jesus Christ our Lord.
> Through him, and with him, and in him,
> by the power of the Holy Spirit,
> with all who stand before you in earth
> and heaven,
> we worship you, Father almighty,
> in songs of everlasting praise:
> Blessing and honour and glory and power
> be yours for ever and ever. Amen.'[14]

The very dynamic of the Eucharistic Prayer involves us

in the life and being of God. As we are aware that we owe our being to the Father himself, and as we allow the Spirit to breathe his life into us, so we begin to know ourselves as participating in a rhythm of love in which all things are grounded, and whose presence is made known in Christ. As we consent to become part of this rhythm so Christ is realised in us.. The Christ whose presence is known in bread and wine is the Christ whose presence is known in Jesus, whose presence is known in ourselves and in each other, and whose presence is known in the whole of creation. In the silent attentiveness of the moment which follows the end of the Eucharistic Prayer the presence of Christ is known to transcend everything, and yet to fill everything, and to embrace everything. In the complete attentiveness to the presence of Christ in the silence of that moment we are transported into eternity, and the presence of Christ is realised in us, too. The total and undivided attention to the present moment, wherever we may be, and with whatever we may be involved, reveals Christ to be present.

The God-given impulse to realise Christ in ourselves is fulfilled as we respond to the invitation to eat and drink his sacramental Body and Blood. In Christ God is to be present at every level of our being, body, mind and spirit. In the eating and drinking God and creation are known to be part of each other in the mystery of Christ. In the depths of our being God dances his love in us, and the mystery of life in Christ is realised. Here and now, in the present moment, we participate in the silence of eternity, not an empty silence, but one which is vibrant with the presence of love, given and received between Father and Son in the Spirit. In the silence and stillness of eternity the love of God dances.

A PRAYER

Come Holy Spirit,
Take possession of us, and fill us with your life.
Let Christ be formed and brought to birth in us;
In and through him lead us to the Father.
Draw us ever more deeply into the eternal dance of love;
For with the Father and the Son
You are one God,
Worshipped and adored
For ever and ever.

Notes

My Dancing Day
1. The identity of the author is unknown. The carol itself appears in a collection made by William Sandys (1792-1874) and published in London in 1833, entitled: *Christmas Carols Ancient and Modern, including the most popular in the West of England and the airs to which they are sung*. It is thought that *My Dancing Day* may be Cornish in origin.

Introduction
1. John Gardner: *Tomorrow shall be my dancing day*, O.U.P., 1966

Chapter 1: Seeing
1. Genesis 2: 16–17
2. Genesis 3: 4–8
3. Hebrews 11: 1 and 3
4. John 1: 38–39
5. John 1: 36
6. John 1:18
7. John 14: 9b
8. John 20: 25
9. John 1:14

Chapter 2: Enfleshing
1. Genesis 1-2:4a
2. Psalm 8:3–5
3. Psalm 148:13
4. Genesis 1:3
5. Genesis 2:4b–end
6. Genesis 2:7
7. Psalm 104: 29–30

8. Acts 17:24–28
9. Romans 7:19–24
10. John 20:21–22
11. 2 Corinthians 5:17–18
12. Colossians 1:15–17
13. John 1:1–4,14
14. 2 Corinthians 5:17

Chapter 3: Consenting

1. John 1: 10–13
2. Philippians 2: 5–11
3. 2 Corinthians 8:9
4. Matthew 7: 13–14
5. Luke 5:11–32
6. Romans 8:38–39
7. Acts 9:1–22
8. Acts 9:17–19
9. Galatians 2:19–20
10. Philippians 3:7–9

Chapter 4: Inspiring

1. Job 1:21
2. Luke 1:35
3. Mark 1:9–11
4. Galatians 4:6
5. Luke 2:41–52
6. E.g. Matthew 21:23–27; 22:15–22
7. John 14:6
8. Luke 9:23–25
9. Jeremiah 1:4–5
10. Galatians 1:15
11. Ephesians 1:3–12

Chapter 5: Withdrawing

1. Romans 8: 26–27
2. Romans 12:1–2
3. 1 Corinthians 6:19–20

4. Matthew 4: 1–11. See also Mark 1:12–13; Luke 4:1–13
5. Hebrews 4:15-16

Chapter 6: Religionising

1. Luke 4:18–19
2. John 10:10
3. Matthew 4:8–10
4. Matthew 4:23–25
5. Matthew 9:2–8; Mark 2:1–12; Luke 5:17–26
6. Mark 2:5
7. Mark 2:7
8. Matthew 11:2–6
9. Matthew 12:38–41
10. Matthew 26:59–66; Mark 14:55–64
11. Matthew 12: 6
12. Matthew 9:10–11
13. Matthew 9:14
14. Matthew 12:9–14
15. Matthew 15:1–2
16. Matthew 15: 9
17. Matthew 23:13
18. Deuteronomy 30: 19–20
19. Mark 12: 28–34
20. John 3:2
21. John 3: 3,6
22. John 3:8

Chapter 7: Trusting

1. Hebrews 11:8
2. Mark 1:16–20
3. Mark 3:19
4. Matthew 19:21–22
5. John 12:6
6. Mark 2:17
7. John 7:32
8. Matthew 27:3–5

9. Matthew 26:75
10. Matthew 26:38–39
11. Luke 22:44
12. Matthew 13:44–45
13. Matthew 26:39

Chapter 8: Suffering
1. Mark 14:63–65
2. Mark 15:16–20
3. Mark 15:29–32
4. Mark 15:34
5. Philippians 3:10–11
6. Romans 6:5
7. Colossians 1:24–26

Chapter 9: Dying
1. Genesis 3:1–5
2. 1 Corinthians 15:21–22;26
3. Luke 23:34
4. John 19:26–27
5. Matthew 27:46; Mark 15:34

Chapter 10: Rising
1. Mark 16:1–2
2. John 20:1
3. Matthew 28:1
4. Luke 24:1
5. Mark 16:6–7
6. Mark 16:8
7. Matthew 28:8
8. Matthew 28:9–10
9. Luke 24:15–16
10. Luke 24:30–32
11. John 20:11–14
12. John 20:16–18
13. John 20:27–29
14. John 21:15–17
15. Colossians 1:15–18

Chapter 11: Realising

1. Revelation 21:1–5
2. Revelation 21:9–11, 22–24
3. Matthew 22:1–2
4. John 4:1–26
5. John 4:7
6. John 4:15
7. John 4:21–24
8. John 4:25
9. John 4:26
10. The Alternative Service Book 1980, First Eucharistic Prayer, p. 130
11. Ibid
12. ASB p. 131
13. Ibid
14. ASB p. 132